PRIMROSE BAKERY
EVERYDAY

MARTHA SWIFT

PRIMROSE BAKERY

EVERYDAY

◩ SQUARE PEG

For Ray

CONTENTS

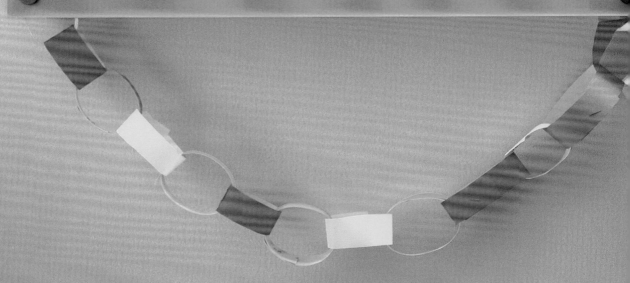

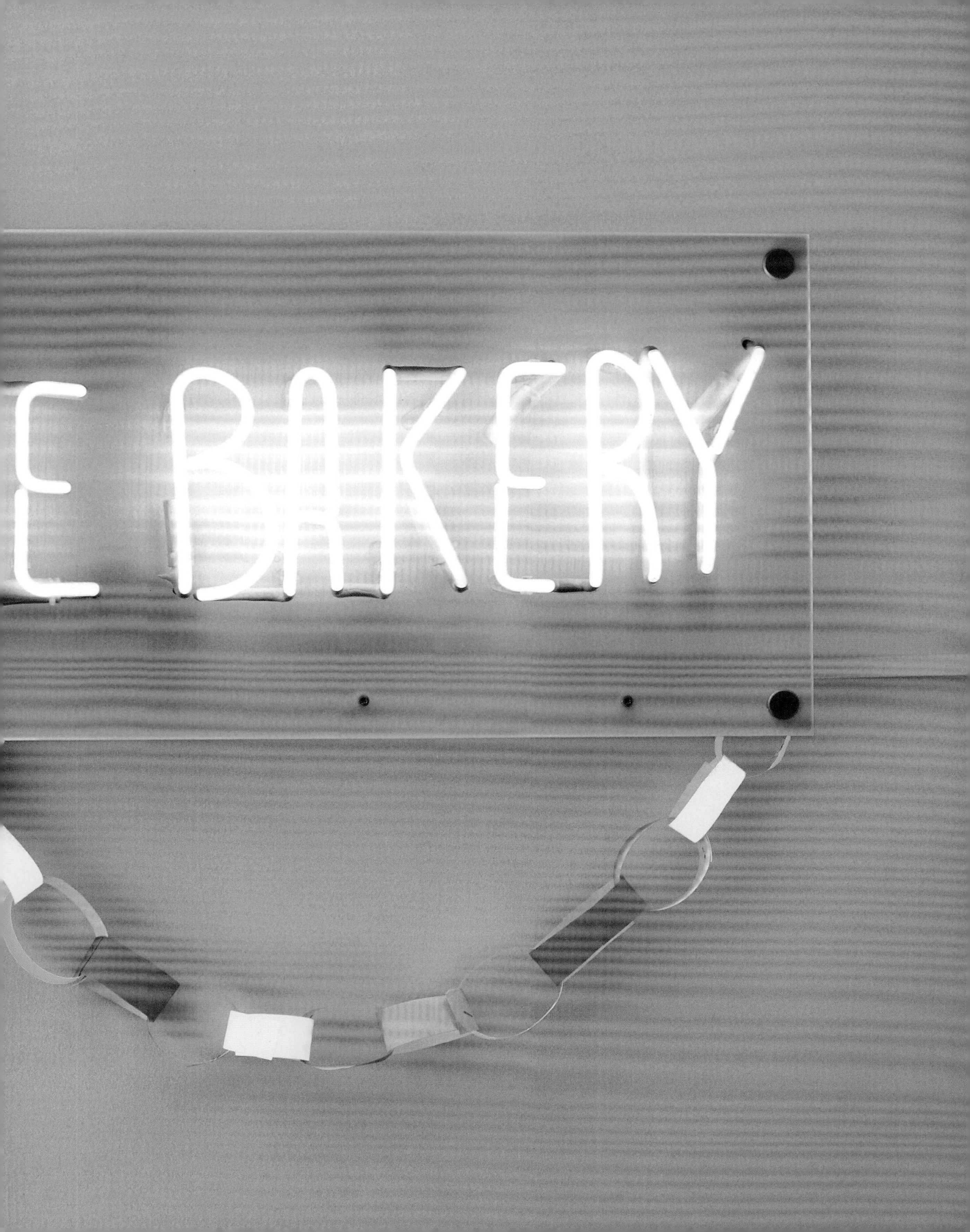
E BAKERY

INTRODUCTION

Primrose Bakery Everyday is the bakery's fifth cookbook, all of them written since *Cupcakes from the Primrose Bakery* was published in 2009. I hope that our loyal fans who have followed the growth of the bakery since its early days will find this new book as enjoyable and useful as the others and appreciate that they are all designed to complement each other. And if this is your first Primrose Bakery book, I hope you will enjoy the wide range of exciting and varied recipes as well as the snapshot of daily life at our two bakeries that it provides.

There are a few recipes which have been repeated from one book to the next and this is simply so that the reader has the complete recipe to hand without the need to check previous books. It also shows how easy it is to adapt and make minimal changes to a recipe and end up with something completely different.

It is always a pleasure to work on a new book as it gives all of us at the bakery an opportunity to come up with, and test new recipes. As with all the other Primrose Bakery books, I only include a recipe if I am confident and happy enough to sell the end product in my shops. We test every recipe thoroughly, taking into account the taste, look, ease of preparation and availability of ingredients. Having started the bakery as a home business, I want to ensure that all the recipes are easy to follow at home. All the recipes in our books are made and then sold at our two bakeries on a regular basis, whether it be every day, once a month or on certain occasions throughout the year. We only introduce a new recipe when we all feel it is good enough, and we are lucky to have many loyal customers to give us feedback and ideas.

I always recommend that you buy the best ingredients you can afford – baking doesn't usually involve too many different ingredients, so if you can buy the best-quality ones, it makes a real difference. The key ingredients I would recommend spending a bit more money on, if possible, are free-range or organic eggs, a high-quality vanilla extract and unsalted butter. Before you start to prepare any of these recipes, it is usually beneficial to have all the ingredients at room temperature. So maybe just take the butter, eggs and milk out of the fridge while you get everything else ready. If you do want to invest in some specialist culinary equipment, I would suggest a sugar thermometer and a cook's blowtorch, both of which we use in some of our recipes. These are not absolutely essential, just something you may want to consider buying. A good electric hand mixer and a food processor, however, are pretty much indispensable for easy and enjoyable baking. We still rely heavily on both these items, as everything at the bakery is made and iced by hand. We go through an impressive amount of hand mixers, sometimes up to three a month, but couldn't manage without them as they always seem to give the best results, even when we're baking huge quantities.

The last year at the bakery has been a busy one. We invested in our first delivery van, a very sweet, tiny Megavan, with our logo on the side, which not only allows us to deliver our cakes in and around London, but also to sell directly from it by opening it up at the side. We took the van to the Lovebox Festival in London in July 2014 and to several food events, such as Feast at Tobacco Dock in east London and the Street Dots food market in the City. It is always great to meet other food sellers and to take our cakes out and about. We also set up stalls at the Manchester Cake and Bake show in April 2014, at Taste of London in Regents Park in June 2014 and 2015, at Jamie Oliver's Big Feastival in the Cotswolds in August 2014 and 2015, and at the BBC Good Food Bakes and Cakes show in north London in October 2014. There are some incredible small food producers and businesses in the UK right now and it is an honour to be part of this growing trend and to meet other like-minded and passionate business people. It is also lovely to get out and meet all of our amazing customers and fans – and this is one of the reasons I love doing this job so much.

I am hoping to open a third Primrose Bakery in the near future, and perhaps a fourth, but need to be sure that the location is right and that at no time do we compromise on the quality of our cakes and our customer service. The bakery is only as good as the last cake that has gone out of the door and, while I can't imagine doing any other job, it is often challenging to make a small food business a success and to maintain that success. I want to be certain that all our cakes are of the highest quality at all times, both in taste and presentation, and this gets harder the bigger a business gets.

I have often said before how we all work together at the bakery as a team, with as many staff as wish to being involved in the books. To work with such a talented team of chefs and shop staff makes my job such a pleasure. Again, this book has been achieved with the invaluable help of the bakery's former head chef, Lisa Chan, and it is always inspiring to work with someone who has such a love of cooking and recipe development. The bakery's current head chef, Daniel, has also been very involved in the creation of new recipes and he leads a small but amazing team of pastry chefs in the two bakery kitchens. Our business manager, Sally,

and her deputy, Rachel, are such key parts of the business that it is hard to imagine Primrose Bakery without them or, indeed, our former manager Faye and the other dedicated shop staff, including my eldest daughter, Daisy, who has been so fantastic both at working in the shop and helping me with the business.

I hope you enjoy reading and using this book as much as we have enjoyed producing it. And I hope it gives you a real insight into what it is like to work at and run a small food business and that, through our recipes, you can see how much we love to create new and exciting cakes that, in turn, we can pass on to you to bake at home.

Spring is probably the most hopeful time of year, when the days are getting longer, the trees are sprouting new leaves and the blossom is out. After a long winter, it's nice to finally turn a corner and start thinking of the year ahead. At Primrose Bakery we know spring is on its way when the chefs start arriving at and leaving work in the daylight. The two big Primrose Bakery occasions in spring are Valentine's Day (although, of course, as we all know, spring doesn't start officially until March) and Easter, so in this chapter you will find some recipes specific to these, as well as plenty of recipes that would work as teatime treats or as a brunch or breakfast.

BAKEWELL SLICE

The famous English tart, with its distinctive jam filling and almond taste, originated from Derbyshire in the 1800s and seemed a natural to turn into a slice. This would best be made in the late spring/early summer when the first British raspberries come into season.

Makes one 33×23cm tray, serving 15

RASPBERRY BASE

300g plain flour
90g soft light brown sugar
65g ground almonds
188g unsalted butter, softened
150g raspberry jam
200g fresh or frozen raspberries,
defrosted if frozen

- Preheat the oven to 180°C/160°C (fan)/ 350°F/gas mark 4. Lightly grease a 33×23cm baking tray and line with parchment paper.
- Put the flour, sugar and ground almonds into a bowl and stir to combine. Add the softened butter and, using an electric hand mixer, beat until well combined and the mixture has a crumb-like consistency.
- Press this mixture evenly into the base of the baking tray and bake on the middle rack of the oven for 10–15 minutes, or until golden brown on top and firm to the touch.
- Remove from the oven (leave the oven on) and allow to cool for 10–15 minutes before spreading with the raspberry jam and scattering the fresh raspberries over the top. Set aside while you prepare the frangipane filling.

→

FRANGIPANE FILLING

125g unsalted butter
125g golden caster sugar
1 large egg
150g ground almonds
½ teaspoon almond extract
a handful of flaked almonds, for sprinkling on top

- In a bowl, cream the butter and sugar together until light and fluffy, using an electric hand mixer. Add the egg and mix until just combined. Add the ground almonds and almond extract and beat again.
- Carefully spread this mixture evenly over the raspberry base and sprinkle some flaked almonds over the top.
- Return the tray to the oven and bake for 35–40 minutes, or until an inserted skewer comes out clean. If the top starts to brown too quickly, cover with a piece of kitchen foil until the slice is cooked through.
- Leave to cool slightly while you prepare the glaze.

GLAZE

60g icing sugar
1 tablespoon water

- Mix the icing sugar and water together in a bowl, using an electric hand mixer or a wooden spoon, until you have a smooth glaze with a coating consistency.
- Once the slice is almost cool, drizzle the glaze in diagonals across the whole slice. Allow it to set and then cut as desired to serve. Keep any uneaten slice in an airtight container at room temperature for 3–4 days.

BANOFFEE LOAF

We sometimes turn our cupcake flavours into loaves, and this has been one of our most successful. It's hard to resist the combination of caramel and banana in any form. A homemade loaf cake always makes a nice teatime treat and it's also good as a picnic snack or a thank-you gift when you are invited for a meal.

Makes one 900g loaf, serving 8–10

BANANA LOAF

190g plain flour
1½ teaspoons baking powder
95g unsalted butter, softened
190g golden caster sugar
2 large eggs
1 teaspoon vanilla extract
3 ripe bananas, mashed

- Preheat the oven to 180°C/160°C (fan)/350°F/gas mark 4. Lightly grease a 900g loaf tin and line with parchment paper or a loaf tin liner.
- Combine the flour and baking powder in a bowl and set aside.
- In a separate bowl, cream the butter and sugar together until light and fluffy, using an electric hand mixer. Add the eggs one at a time, making sure the first one is well incorporated before adding the second. Add the vanilla extract with the second egg. Add the mashed bananas and mix until they are well incorporated (the riper the banana the better the end result).
- Finally, add the flour mixture and beat until well incorporated and you have a smooth batter.
- Pour the batter into the lined loaf tin and bake for 45–60 minutes, or until the loaf is golden brown and an inserted skewer comes out clean. Allow the loaf to cool in its tin before turning it out onto a wire rack to cool completely.
- While the loaf is cooling, make the salted caramel icing.

SALTED CARAMEL BUTTERCREAM ICING

75g unsalted butter, softened
75g Salted Caramel Sauce (see recipe on page 244 and make half the quantity of sauce)
150g icing sugar

- In a bowl, beat the butter and caramel sauce together until smooth, using an electric hand mixer. Add the icing sugar and beat on a low speed until fully incorporated, then beat for a further 30–60 seconds on a medium speed until the mixture is smooth and lump-free.

ASSEMBLE

banana chips, to decorate

- Ice the top of the cooled loaf with the salted caramel buttercream icing and decorate with a line of dried banana chips along the centre.
- Keep any uneaten loaf in an airtight container at room temperature for 3–4 days.

BOURBON BISCUIT CUPCAKES

We created these cupcakes at the same time as our Custard Cream Cupcakes
on page 30 and they are just as popular. We have always loved Bourbon
biscuits at Primrose Bakery and in fact make our own version, as some of our readers
will know from previous books. For these cupcakes, however, we
have used the classic Bourbon biscuit, which was first baked in Britain in 1910.

Makes 19 regular-sized cupcakes

CHOCOLATE SPONGE

185g plain flour
¾ teaspoon baking powder
¾ teaspoon bicarbonate of soda
a pinch of salt
250ml milk
1 teaspoon vanilla extract
115g dark chocolate (70% cocoa solids),
broken into small pieces
85g unsalted butter
175g soft light brown sugar
2 large eggs, separated
150g crushed Bourbon biscuits

- Preheat the oven to 180°C/160°C (fan)/350°F/
gas mark 4. Line two 12-hole muffin tins with
19 muffin cases.
- Combine the flour, baking powder, bicarbonate
of soda and salt in a bowl. Pour the milk into a jug
and stir in the vanilla extract. Set these aside.
- Melt the chocolate in a microwaveable or
heatproof bowl, either in the microwave in short
bursts or over a pan of lightly simmering
water, being careful not to let it burn. Set aside
to cool slightly.
- Using an electric hand mixer, cream the butter
and sugar together in another bowl until pale
and fluffy.
- In a separate bowl and with clean beaters,
beat the egg yolks for several minutes. Slowly
add the egg yolks to the creamed butter and
sugar and beat well.

- Pour in the melted chocolate and beat until all
of it is incorporated. Add a third of the flour
mixture and then a third of the milk and vanilla,
and beat on a low speed until just combined.
Repeat until all the flour and milk mixtures
have been incorporated.
- In a clean bowl and with clean beaters, beat
the egg whites until medium peaks form. Gently
fold into the chocolate batter with a metal
spoon, then fold in the crushed Bourbon biscuits.
- Spoon the batter evenly into the muffin cases,
filling each one to about two-thirds full.
- Bake for 20–25 minutes, until the cakes are
firm to the touch and an inserted skewer comes
out clean. Allow the cupcakes to cool in their
tins for about 10 minutes, then turn out onto
a wire rack to cool completely.

CHOCOLATE CUSTARD

3 egg yolks
30g dark chocolate (70% cocoa solids), melted
60g granulated sugar
1 tablespoon plain flour
1½ teaspoons cocoa powder
2½ tablespoons cornflour
185ml whole milk
185ml double cream
1 teaspoon vanilla extract
2 tablespoons unsalted butter, at room temperature

- In a heatproof bowl, whisk together the egg yolks, melted chocolate, sugar, flour, cocoa powder and cornflour until combined.
- Pour the milk and cream into a pan over a low to medium heat and bring to a simmer, being very careful not to let it boil. Slowly pour this over the yolk mixture in a thin stream, whisking continuously.
- Pour the mixture back into the pan through a sieve and bring to the boil on a low to medium heat, stirring constantly until it thickens.
- Pour into a clean bowl, then cover with cling film, placing the cling film directly on top of the mixture to prevent a skin from forming. Allow the chocolate custard to cool, then refrigerate until completely cold.
- Once it's cold, beat in the vanilla extract and butter until you have a smooth consistency.

CHOCOLATE CUSTARD CREAM

250ml double cream
½ batch Chocolate Custard (see left)

- Beat the double cream until you have almost stiff peaks.
- Mix a few tablespoons of the whipped cream into the chocolate custard to soften it, then fold in the remaining whipped cream.

ASSEMBLE

19 Bourbon biscuits, left whole or broken in half, to decorate

- Remove about 2cm of sponge from the centre of each cupcake, using a cupcake corer or a small paring knife. Fill the holes you have created with the remaining chocolate custard so it comes to just under the top of each cupcake.
- Ice the cupcakes with the chocolate custard cream and decorate each one with a whole Bourbon biscuit or two halves.

BREAKFAST MUFFINS

Breakfast has always been important to us at Primrose Bakery. Our hand-rolled croissants were an instant hit with our customers, and occasionally we add something new to our breakfast menu, such as these muffins, which would be a nice way to start the day.

Makes 10 regular-sized muffins

MUFFINS

150g wholemeal flour
60g golden caster sugar
35g rolled oats, plus extra for sprinkling
½ teaspoon bicarbonate of soda
½ teaspoon baking powder
¼ teaspoon salt
½ teaspoon ground cinnamon
40g unsalted butter, melted
80ml vegetable oil
1 large egg
50ml sour cream
90g apple sauce
(from a jar, or purée some apples)
115g fresh or frozen blueberries, defrosted if frozen
50g raw unsalted almonds, roughly chopped

- Preheat the oven to 180°C/160°C (fan)/350°F/ gas mark 4. Line a 12-hole muffin tin with 10 muffin cases and set aside.
- Using a wooden spoon, mix all the dry ingredients together in a bowl, then make a well in the centre.
- Add the melted butter to a separate bowl along with the oil, egg, sour cream and apple sauce and mix together with a wooden spoon. Then pour this mixture into the well in the dry ingredients.
- Using the wooden spoon, gently mix the dry and wet ingredients together until just combined.
- Add the blueberries and almonds and gently mix in.
- Spoon this mixture evenly into the muffin cases, filling each case to about two-thirds full, then sprinkle a few rolled oats over each one.
- Bake for 25–30 minutes, or until the muffins are a light golden brown and an inserted skewer comes out clean. Allow the muffins to cool in their tin for 5–10 minutes before turning out onto a wire rack to continue cooling.
- These are nice eaten while still slightly warm, but, if you prefer, they can be left to cool completely before serving.
- Store any uneaten muffins in an airtight container and eat within 2–3 days.

CREME EGG CUPCAKES

My eldest daughter, Daisy, loved creme eggs when she was little, so these cupcakes always remind me of her and, of course, of Easter, when the famous Cadbury's creme eggs are available to buy for a limited time. We use the mini ones in this recipe and they work perfectly without the cupcakes becoming too sweet.

Makes 12 regular-sized cupcakes

BROWNIE SPONGE

175g unsalted butter
175g dark chocolate (70% cocoa solids), broken into small pieces
200g golden caster sugar
3 large eggs
1 teaspoon vanilla extract
85g self-raising flour

- Preheat the oven to 180°C/160°C (fan)/ 350°F/gas mark 4. Line a 12-hole muffin tin with 12 muffin cases.
- Melt the butter and chocolate together in a microwaveable or heatproof bowl, either in the microwave in short bursts or over a pan of lightly simmering water. Stir the mixture continuously to ensure the chocolate melts completely, then set aside to cool slightly.
- In a separate bowl, beat the sugar, eggs and vanilla extract together, using an electric hand mixer, until pale and fluffy.
- Pour the slightly cooled chocolate mixture into the sugar and egg mixture and gently fold through with a spatula. Sift the flour on top and fold through until well combined.
- Spoon the mixture evenly into the muffin cases, filling each case to about two-thirds full.
- Bake for 15–20 minutes, or until an inserted skewer comes out clean. Allow the cupcakes to stand in their tin for 10–15 minutes before turning out onto a wire rack to cool completely.

MARSHMALLOW ICING

120g granulated sugar
80g golden syrup
1½ tablespoons water
2 large egg whites
½ teaspoon vanilla extract
¼ teaspoon yellow gel food colouring

- Place the sugar, golden syrup and water in a pan and cook on a high heat until the mixture reaches 'soft-ball' stage – this is when the bubbles in the mixture almost start to stick together and the micture would drop off a spoon in a smooth, slow stream. This could take up to 6 minutes.
- In a separate, clean bowl, whisk the egg whites until soft peaks start to form.
- When the sugar mixture has reached soft-ball stage, remove from the heat.
- Using an electric hand mixer on a low speed, pour the hot sugar mixture in a slow, steady stream into the egg whites. Continue to beat on a low speed until all the hot sugar is in the mixing bowl.
- Turn the mixer up to a medium-high speed and continue whipping the mixture until it becomes thick, glossy and cool. Add the vanilla extract towards the end of the mixing process.
- Divide the icing between two bowls and colour one of them with the yellow gel food colouring until the icing becomes a pale egg yellow colour.

Note This icing is easiest to work with while it is still a little warm, so try to use it right away. If you do have some left over, store it in the fridge overnight but we would not recommend keeping it for long.

ASSEMBLE

18 mini creme eggs, unwrapped – keep 12 whole and cut the remaining 6 in half lengthways

- Using a small paring knife or a cupcake corer, remove a small piece of sponge (about 2cm) from the centre of each cupcake.
- Place a whole mini creme egg into each of the holes you have created.
- Ice the top of each cupcake with the white marshmallow icing and then smear a small amount of yellow marshmallow on one side of the white icing. Swirl the icings together with a palette knife to create a marbled effect. Finish by decorating each cupcake with half a mini creme egg placed on top.

CUSTARD CREAM CUPCAKES

The beloved British custard cream biscuit was turned into cupcake form by our chef Mary, and it is now one of our bestselling flavours. These look so pretty and I think you will enjoy them as much as our customers do. The flavour of the biscuits really does come through both in the cupcakes and the icing.

Makes 15 regular-sized cupcakes

CUSTARD CREAM SPONGE

150g self-raising flour
115g plain flour
10g custard powder
120ml semi-skimmed milk, at room temperature
1 teaspoon vanilla extract
110g unsalted butter
225g golden caster sugar
2 large eggs
100g crushed custard cream biscuits

- Preheat the oven to 180°C/160°C (fan)/350°F/gas mark 4. Line two 12-hole muffin tins with 15 muffin cases.
- Combine the flours and custard powder in a bowl. Pour the milk into a jug and stir in the vanilla extract.
- Using an electric hand mixer, cream the butter and sugar together until pale and fluffy. Beat in the eggs one at a time, making sure the first one is well incorporated before adding the second.
- Add a third of the flour mixture and beat on a low speed until just combined, then beat in a third of the milk and vanilla. Repeat until all the flour and milk have been incorporated. Then using a spatula, gently fold in the crushed custard creams.
- Spoon the batter evenly into the muffin cases, filling each case to about two-thirds full.
- Bake for 15–18 minutes, or until the cakes are golden brown on top and an inserted skewer comes out clean. Allow the cupcakes to cool in their tins for 10 minutes, then turn out onto a wire rack to cool completely before decorating.

VANILLA CUSTARD

2 egg yolks
75g granulated sugar
1 teaspoon vanilla extract
1½ tablespoons cornflour
125ml milk
170ml double cream

- In a bowl, whisk together the yolks, sugar, vanilla extract and cornflour until smooth.
- Bring the milk and cream to a simmer in a pan on the hob, being careful not to let it boil. Slowly pour this over the yolk mixture in a thin stream, whisking continuously.
- Pour the mixture back into the pan through a sieve and place on a medium-low heat, stirring constantly until it comes to the boil and is thick.
- Pour into a clean, heatproof bowl and cover with cling film, placing the cling film directly on top of the mixture to prevent a skin from forming. Allow to cool, then refrigerate until set.

VANILLA CUSTARD CREAM

½ batch Vanilla Custard (see left),
at room temperature
300g unsalted butter, at room temperature

<u>Note</u> It is very important that the vanilla custard and butter are at room temperature or the mixture could split.

- Pour the vanilla custard into a bowl. Chop the butter into small squares.
- Start beating the vanilla custard, and add one piece of butter at a time until it is all incorporated and you have a smooth and silky icing.

ASSEMBLE

½ batch Vanilla Custard (see left)
12 custard cream biscuits,
cut or broken neatly in half, to decorate

- Remove about 2cm of sponge from the centre of each cupcake, using a cupcake corer or a small paring knife.
- Fill the holes with the vanilla custard so it comes to just under the surface of each cupcake. Ice with the vanilla custard cream.
- Finish by decorating each cupcake with two halves of a custard cream biscuit.

HOT CROSS BUN CUPCAKES

There are few things that remind us of Easter more than a hot cross bun, preferably toasted and spread with butter. Traditionally, hot cross buns are eaten on Good Friday as part of the Christian celebration, but in reality it is now possible to buy them in the supermarkets during the months leading up to Easter. Our head chef Daniel produced a hot cross bun cupcake for us during Easter 2014 and the spiced cream cheese icing complements the sponge nicely.

Makes 18 regular-sized cupcakes

SPONGE

220g self-raising flour
2 teaspoons ground cinnamon
1 teaspoon ground nutmeg
1 teaspoon ground allspice
¼ teaspoon salt
1 shop-bought hot cross bun, chopped
50ml semi-skimmed milk
160ml sour cream
200g unsalted butter
240g golden caster sugar
2 large eggs
½ teaspoon vanilla extract
60g diced mixed peel
60g currants

- Preheat the oven to 180°C/160°C (fan)/350°F/gas mark 4. Line two 12-hole muffin tins with 18 muffin cases.
- Combine the flour, spices and salt in a bowl and set aside.
- In another bowl, soak the chopped hot cross bun in the milk and sour cream for about 15–20 minutes, until soft.
- Using an electric hand mixer on a medium-high speed, cream the butter and sugar together in a separate bowl until light and fluffy. Add the eggs one at a time, making sure the first one is well incorporated before adding the second. Add the vanilla extract with the second egg.
- Add the flour and spice mixture a third at a time, mixing on a low speed until just combined. Then repeat this process with the soaked hot cross bun mixture. Using a spatula, gently fold in the mixed peel and currants.
- Spoon the batter evenly into the muffin cases, filling each case to about two-thirds full.
- Bake for 15–18 minutes, or until an inserted skewer comes out clean. Allow the cupcakes to cool in their tins for 10 minutes before transferring to wire racks to cool completely.

SPICED CREAM CHEESE ICING

75g unsalted butter
190g cream cheese, softened
600g icing sugar
1 teaspoon ground allspice

- Put all of the ingredients into a bowl and, using an electric hand mixer, beat on a low speed until they just start to come together. Scrape down the sides of the bowl, then increase the speed to medium-high and beat for a further 30–45 seconds, until you have a light and smooth icing.

ASSEMBLE

3 shop-bought hot cross buns, each cut into 6 crouton-sized cubes and lightly toasted in the oven, to decorate

- Ice the cupcakes with the spiced cream cheese icing and top each one with three crouton-sized cubes of hot cross bun.

KEY LIME PIE CUPCAKES

Key lime pie originates from Key West in Florida, which is where the especially sweet key limes come from, although any juicy and ripe limes will work well. The combination of lime and marshmallow is delicious and these cupcakes would make a good dessert.

Makes 12 regular-sized cupcakes

LIME CURD

1 × 397g tin condensed milk
zest and juice of 4 ripe limes
2 large egg yolks
110g golden caster sugar

- In a jug or bowl, whisk together the condensed milk, lime juice, egg yolks and sugar. Pour the mixture into a pan and place over a low heat. Bring to the boil slowly, stirring continuously. This should take 15–20 minutes. Then allow the mixture to simmer gently for a further 5 minutes, stirring continuously, until it thickens slightly.
- Stir through half of the lime zest, then pour the mixture into a small mixing bowl. Set aside the remaining lime zest for decoration.
- Allow the lime curd to cool, then cover with cling film and refrigerate.

VANILLA SPONGE

110g unsalted butter
225g golden caster sugar
2 large eggs
150g self-raising flour
125g plain flour
120ml semi-skimmed milk, at room temperature
1 teaspoon vanilla extract

- Preheat the oven to 180°C/160°C (fan)/ 350°F/gas mark 4. Line a 12-hole muffin tin with 12 muffin cases.
- In a large mixing bowl, cream together the butter and sugar until pale and smooth, which should take 3–5 minutes with an electric hand mixer. Add the eggs one at a time, beating for a few minutes after each addition.
- Combine the two flours in a separate bowl. Pour the milk into a jug and stir in the vanilla extract.
- Add a third of the flours to the creamed butter mixture and beat well. Pour in a third of the milk and vanilla extract and beat again. Repeat until all the flour and milk have been added.
- Carefully spoon the mixture into the muffin cases, filling each case to about two-thirds full.
- Bake for 20–25 minutes, or until the cakes are golden brown on top and have risen slightly.
- Allow to cool in their tin for 10 minutes, then remove to a wire rack to cool completely before icing.

→

MARSHMALLOW ICING

- Make up one batch of marshmallow icing, following the icing recipe for Creme Egg Cupcakes on page 29, but omit the yellow food colouring.

ASSEMBLE

reserved lime zest

- Scoop out about 2cm of sponge from the centre of each cupcake with a cupcake corer or small paring knife. Fill each hole with lime curd so it comes to the top of the cupcake.
- Ice the cupcakes with the marshmallow icing and sprinkle a pinch of lime zest on top of each cake.
- These cupcakes are best eaten on the day they are made as the marshmallow icing looks and tastes better when used immediately.

MAPLE AND BACON CUPCAKES

Now here is a flavour you will either love or hate! Strange as it may sound, these cakes are truly delicious, so do give them a try even if you are not quite sure about the flavour. The idea came from some maple- and bacon-flavoured popcorn that tasted great, so it seemed logical to try it as a cupcake flavour. If you're still not convinced, try the maple and blueberry variation instead, which I guess is our vegetarian version of these cupcakes!

Makes 12 regular-sized cupcakes

CANDIED BACON

120g streaky bacon strips
3 tablespoons golden caster sugar

- Preheat the oven to 180°C/160°C (fan)/350°F/ gas mark 4. Lightly grease a baking tray and line with parchment paper.
- Lay the strips of bacon on the lined tray and sprinkle with the sugar. Bake for 15–20 minutes, or until the bacon is golden brown and crispy.
- Allow to cool on the tray while you prepare the cake batter. Leave the oven on.

SPONGE

115g unsalted butter, softened
160ml maple syrup, plus extra for brushing on top
50g soft light brown sugar
2 large eggs
230g self-raising flour
160ml buttermilk (or 140ml milk and juice of 1 lemon)
60g Candied Bacon (see left)

- Line a 12-hole muffin tin with 12 muffin cases.
- In a bowl, cream the butter, maple syrup and brown sugar together with an electric hand mixer until light and fluffy.
- Add the eggs one at a time, making sure the first one is well incorporated before adding the second. Add the flour and beat until it all just starts to come together.
- Pour in the buttermilk (or milk and lemon juice) and mix until well combined and smooth. Finely dice the cooked bacon and fold it into the batter. Set aside the rest of the bacon strips for decoration.
- Spoon the batter evenly into the muffin cases, filling each case to about two-thirds full.
- Bake for 18–20 minutes, or until the cakes are golden brown on top and an inserted skewer comes out clean. Allow to stand in their tin for 15 minutes before turning out onto a wire rack to cool.
- Once the cupcakes have cooled, brush each one with a thin covering of maple syrup.

MAPLE SYRUP BUTTERCREAM ICING

160g unsalted butter, softened
500g icing sugar
80ml maple syrup

- Put all the ingredients into a bowl and mix together on a low speed with an electric hand mixer. Once all the ingredients are combined, scrape down the sides of the bowl and then mix for a further 30–60 seconds on a medium speed until the icing is smooth and lump-free.

ASSEMBLE

about 60g Candied Bacon (see page 42), cut into bite-sized pieces

- Ice each cupcake with the maple syrup icing and decorate with bite-sized pieces of candied bacon.

Variation
Makes 12 regular–sized cupcakes

MAPLE AND BLUEBERRY CUPCAKES

- Make the cake batter, following the above sponge recipe but leaving out the bacon. Then once you have spooned the batter into the muffin cases, push 4–5 blueberries into each one. Bake as above and leave to cool before brushing with maple syrup.
- Ice each cupcake with the maple syrup icing and decorate with a few extra blueberries.

MAPLE BANANA LOAF WITH BUTTERSCOTCH GLAZE

This loaf came about as a collaboration between my eldest daughter, Daisy, and our former head chef, Lisa Chan. One of the best things was that it meant we had plenty of sample cakes to try as they worked on different ways to perfect it. I'm sure you will agree it is very to eat several slices.

Makes one 900g loaf, serving 8–10

MAPLE BANANA LOAF

250g self-raising flour
1 teaspoon baking powder
½ teaspoon ground cinnamon
a pinch of salt
110g unsalted butter
150g soft light brown sugar
2 large eggs
60ml maple syrup
1 teaspoon vanilla extract
3 very ripe bananas, mashed
75ml sour cream

- Preheat the oven to 180°C/160°C (fan)/350°F/ gas mark 4. Lightly grease a 900g loaf tin and line with parchment paper or a loaf tin liner.
- Combine the flour, baking powder, cinnamon and salt in a bowl and set aside.
- Using an electric hand mixer on a medium speed, cream the butter and sugar together until light and fluffy. Add the eggs one at a time, beating well after each addition. Pour in the maple syrup and vanilla extract with the second egg, beating everything together until well combined.
- Add the mashed bananas and beat again.
- Add the flour mixture and beat on a low speed until all the ingredients just come together. Add the sour cream and mix until fully incorporated.

- Pour the batter into the prepared loaf tin.
- Bake on the middle rack of the oven for 45–50 minutes, or until the loaf is golden brown on top and an inserted skewer comes out clean.
- Allow the loaf to cool in its tin for 15 minutes before turning out onto a wire rack to continue cooling while you make the glaze.

BUTTERSCOTCH GLAZE

35ml maple syrup
95g soft light brown sugar
50g unsalted butter
2 tablespoons double cream
a pinch of salt

- Put all the ingredients into a small pan and place over a low to medium heat until the butter and sugar have dissolved. Stir regularly.
- Increase the heat to medium-high and bring the mixture up to the boil. Then turn the heat down to medium and allow the mixture to simmer for 2–3 minutes until thick and syrup-like.
- Pour the warm glaze over the still-warm loaf, then allow it to cool and set before cutting the loaf into slices.

MUESLI BARS

These muesli bars keep well, so you could make them in advance and save for a special occasion or just have one or two at a time as a mid-morning snack or in a packed lunch. Our bakery manager, Sally, was pregnant while we were developing these and we often found her with a few on her desk to keep her going through the day.

Makes one 33×23cm tray, giving 20 bars

TOASTED MUESLI

200g rolled oats
70g bran cereal sticks
50g sesame seeds
50g desiccated coconut
120g sunflower seeds
150g assorted nuts (such as macadamia, pecans, almonds), roughly chopped
220g dried fruit (such as pineapple, mango, papaya, apricots), cut into bite-sized pieces

- Put all the ingredients except the dried fruit into a large, deep frying pan or large saucepan. Place over a low to medium heat, stirring constantly to prevent the mixture from burning. Cook for about 10–12 minutes until the mixture is aromatic and toasted.
- Pour the mixture into a large mixing bowl. Add the chopped-up dried fruit and stir through until well combined. Set this aside while you prepare the honey syrup.

HONEY SYRUP

130ml honey
60g soft light brown sugar
130g unsalted butter
a pinch of salt
2 tablespoons maple syrup
35ml golden syrup

- Preheat the oven to 180°C/160°C (fan)/350°F/ gas mark 4. Lightly grease the bottom and sides of a 33×23cm baking tray and line with parchment paper. Set aside.
- Heat all the ingredients in a small pan over a low heat until the butter has melted and the sugar has dissolved. Turn up the heat and bring the mixture to the boil, then turn down the heat and allow it to simmer for 2–3 minutes until thick and golden brown.
- Pour the honey syrup directly over the toasted muesli and mix together thoroughly with a wooden spoon until the muesli is well coated with the syrup.
- Pour this mixture into the lined baking tray, then spread it out evenly and push it into the corners of the tray. Lightly push the mixture down with the back of the wooden spoon to flatten and compress it.
- Bake for 20–25 minutes, until golden brown on top.
- Allow to cool completely in the tray before transferring to a board and cutting into pieces.
- These bars can be stored in an airtight container for up to a week.

SPRINKLE COOKIES

These fun, colourful cookies would be great to make with children one afternoon, although you might then eat them all in one sitting!

Makes 15 cookies

COOKIES

200g plain flour
1 teaspoon baking powder
½ teaspoon bicarbonate of soda
1 teaspoon cream of tartar
¼ teaspoon salt
115g unsalted butter
150g granulated sugar
1 large egg
2 teaspoons vanilla extract
50–60g sprinkles (such as hundreds and thousands)

- Lightly grease two baking trays and line with parchment paper.
- Combine the flour, baking powder, bicarbonate of soda, cream of tartar and salt in a bowl and set aside.
- Using an electric hand mixer, cream the butter and sugar together in another bowl until light and fluffy. Add the egg and vanilla extract and mix until combined.
- On a low speed, add the flour mixture a third at a time, until thoroughly mixed in. Pour in the sprinkles and mix until they are evenly distributed. Allow the dough to rest in the fridge for 15–20 minutes.
- Preheat the oven to 180°C/160°C (fan)/350°F/gas mark 4.
- Divide the dough into 15 portions, then roll into balls and place on the lined baking trays, leaving a gap of about 3cm between each one to allow room for them to spread during baking. Gently press each ball down with the back of a spoon to flatten them into disc shapes about 1cm thick.
- Bake for 10–15 minutes, checking halfway through and rotating the trays, until the cookies just start to brown at the edges.
- Allow to cool on their trays for 2 minutes before removing to wire racks to cool completely.

RED BERRY BROWNIE

I usually recommend using fresh fruit where possible, but these gooey brownies also work well with frozen berries, and the chocolate and red fruit look so pretty together.

Makes one 33×23cm tray, serving 15

BROWNIE

250g unsalted butter
250g golden caster sugar
40g cocoa powder
150g plain flour
¼ teaspoon baking powder
300g white chocolate chips
3 large eggs, lightly beaten
200g fresh or frozen red berries, defrosted if frozen

- Preheat the oven to 180°C/160°C (fan)/350°F/ gas mark 4. Lightly grease a 33 × 23cm baking tray and line with parchment paper.
- Melt the butter in the microwave or in a small pan on the hob. Set aside to cool slightly.
- Put the sugar, cocoa, flour and baking powder into a bowl, then add the chocolate chips and stir to combine with a wooden spoon.
- Pour the melted butter into the dry ingredients and stir until well combined. Add the eggs one at a time, making sure each one is well incorporated before adding the next, then stir until well combined.
- Add the red berries and gently fold them into the mixture.
- Pour the batter into the prepared tray and spread it out evenly.
- Bake on the middle rack of the oven for 30–35 minutes. An inserted skewer should come out sticky. This is a fudgey brownie, so it should still be fairly soft to the touch. It's important not to overbake these brownies or they will dry out.
- Allow to cool before cutting into squares.
- These will keep well (at least 3–4 days) if stored in an airtight container.

STRAWBERRY AND APRICOT BATTENBERG CAKE

Please allow a little bit of extra time and patience when making this cake,
but definitely give it a go. Wait until you can buy some fresh
seasonal strawberries too, as they really do taste so much better than frozen ones.

Makes one 20cm two-layer cake, serving 10–12

SPONGE

150g strawberry purée (see below) plus ⅛ teaspoon
pink gel food colouring
200g apricot purée (see below) plus ¼ teaspoon
yellow gel food colouring
300g self-raising flour
½ teaspoon baking powder
¼ teaspoon salt
250g unsalted butter
200g golden caster sugar
3 large eggs
½ teaspoon vanilla extract

- To make the strawberry purée for the sponge and the jam, wash and hull enough strawberries to give you 190g of prepared fruit. Put the strawberries into a food processor bowl and blitz until puréed. Transfer 150g of the strawberry purée (reserve 40g for the jam) to a bowl and add the pink food colouring.
- Repeat this process with the apricots (you can use fresh or tinned – if using fresh, remove the skin and stones first), using enough apricots to give you 240g of prepared fruit. Transfer 200g of the apricot purée (reserve 40g for the jam) to a separate bowl and add the yellow food colouring.
- Preheat the oven to 180°C/160°C (fan)/350°F/ gas mark 4. Grease two 20cm sandwich tins and line with parchment paper.
- Combine the flour, baking powder and salt in a bowl and set aside.

- Using an electric hand mixer, cream the butter and sugar together in a bowl until light and fluffy. Add the eggs one at a time, beating well after each addition. Add the vanilla extract with the last egg.
- Add the flour mixture and mix until just combined. Pour half of this batter into a separate bowl.
- In one of the bowls, carefully fold in the strawberry purée until combined, then pour this into one of the prepared sandwich tins and spread it out evenly. Repeat this process with the remaining batter and the apricot purée, and pour into the second cake tin.
- Bake in the oven for 20–25 minutes, or until the cakes are firm to the touch and an inserted skewer comes out clean.
- Allow the cakes to cool in their tins for 10 minutes before turning out onto wire racks to cool completely.

→

JAM

reserved 40g strawberry purée
reserved 40g apricot purée
20g golden caster sugar
juice of ½ lemon

- Put the purées, sugar and lemon juice into
a small pan over a low to medium heat and
stir constantly until the mixture begins to
boil. Turn the heat down to low and continue
to cook until the mixture becomes thick and
with the consistency of jam. This will take
3–5 minutes. Remove from the heat and allow
to cool.

ALMOND BUTTERCREAM ICING

120g unsalted butter, softened
75g marzipan, softened
300g icing sugar
½ teaspoon almond extract
2–3 tablespoons milk

- Place the butter and marzipan in a bowl,
breaking up the marzipan into small pieces.
Using an electric hand mixer, beat these together
until well combined. Add the icing sugar, almond
extract and milk, and mix on a low speed for
30 seconds, then scrape down the sides of the
bowl and mix for a further minute until all the
ingredients are well combined.

ASSEMBLE

- Cut out two circles of parchment paper, one 15cm in diameter and the other 10cm in diameter.
- Place the 15cm template in the middle of the first cake – pin it down with pins or toothpicks if you wish. Using a sharp knife, carefully cut around this template to make a 15cm round. Do the same with the 10cm template, placing it in the middle of the 15cm round and cutting around it to make a 10cm round. Repeat this process with the second cake.
- Carefully lift the 15cm outer rings from each cake and set to one side.

- Spread a thin layer of jam around the outer edges of the newly created 15cm and 10cm rounds. This will act as a 'glue' to hold the sponge together.
- Now carefully place the 15cm outer rings back in the cakes, but put the strawberry ring into the apricot cake and vice versa. Spread a thin layer of jam on top of one of the cakes, then place the second cake on top.
- To finish, cover the top and sides of the whole cake with the marzipan icing. When you cut into it, you will see the classic checkered Battenberg effect.

LEMON THYME LOAF WITH A YOGHURT DRIZZLE

Loaf cakes have always been popular at Primrose Bakery, so here is a completely new flavour for you to try. The fresh citrus and herb flavours make this cake a good choice to have at teatime or with a morning coffee or brunch.

Makes one 900g loaf, serving 8–10

LEMON THYME SUGAR

20g fresh mint leaves
6g fresh lemon thyme leaves
50g golden caster sugar

- Place the mint, lemon thyme and sugar in a food processor bowl and pulse for about 30 seconds, or until it resembles a fine green sugar.

YOGHURT DRIZZLE

80ml natural Greek yoghurt
½ teaspoon fresh lemon juice
45g icing sugar, sifted

- Place all the ingredients in a bowl and beat together until smooth. Set aside in the fridge until the loaf has cooled completely.

LEMON THYME LOAF

230g self-raising flour
a pinch of salt
70ml lemon juice
70ml milk
210g unsalted butter
180g golden caster sugar
76g lemon thyme sugar
2 large eggs
zest of 1½ lemons

- Preheat the oven to 180°C/160°C (fan)/350°F/ gas mark 4. Lightly grease a 900g loaf tin and line with parchment paper or a loaf tin liner.
- Combine the flour and salt in a bowl. Pour the lemon juice and milk into a jug. Set aside.
- Put the butter and sugars into another bowl and, using an electric hand mixer, cream together until light and fluffy. Add the eggs one at a time, beating well after each addition. Add the lemon zest with the second egg. Add the flour and mix until just combined. Pour in the lemon milk mixture and mix until well combined.
- Pour the batter into the lined loaf tin and bake on the middle rack of the oven for 50–60 minutes, or until the loaf is golden brown and an inserted skewer comes out clean.
- Allow the loaf to cool in its tin for 15 minutes before turning out onto a wire rack to cool.
- Drizzle the yoghurt icing over the top of the loaf, just before serving.

TEACAKES

Our teacakes are based on the famous Tunnock's teacakes with their biscuit base and marshmallow and chocolate topping. Our assistant manager, Rachel, has come up with a few variations for you to try.

Makes about 15 teacakes

EQUIPMENT

a half sphere/hemisphere 40mm diameter
silicone mould
a 4cm cookie cutter
two small piping bags, one with a small round
plastic tip and one with a medium round tip
a sugar thermometer

VANILLA BISCUITS

85g unsalted butter
100g golden caster sugar
1 large egg
½ teaspoon vanilla extract
200g plain flour
½ teaspoon baking powder
¼ teaspoon salt

- Using an electric hand mixer, cream the butter and sugar together in a bowl, then add the egg and vanilla extract. Add the flour, baking powder and salt and mix until it all comes together. Wrap the dough in cling film and place in the fridge for about 20 minutes to rest.
- Preheat the oven to 180°C/160°C (fan)/350°F/ gas mark 4. Lightly grease two baking trays and line with parchment paper.
- On a floured work surface, roll out the dough to about 5mm thick. Using a 4cm cookie cutter, cut into about 15 circles and place on the prepared baking trays, leaving a gap of about 3cm between each one to allow room for the biscuits to spread during baking.

- Bake for 5–8 minutes, until the biscuits are a light golden brown and firm to the touch. They will cook quickly, so keep an eye on the cooking time, and they will also continue to cook a little once they are out of the oven. Leave to cool on wire racks.

Note Any leftover dough can be wrapped tightly in cling film and refrigerated for up to 3 days.

CHOCOLATE MOULDS

250g dark, milk or caramel chocolate chips

- Place three-quarters of the chocolate chips (about 188g) into a microwaveable or heatproof bowl and melt it, either in the microwave in short bursts or over a pan of lightly simmering water, stirring frequently to avoid burning or scorching the chocolate. Once the chocolate has melted and is warm, add the remaining chocolate chips and stir until all the chocolate has melted and is smooth. Allow to cool and thicken slightly.
- Spoon 1 teaspoon of melted chocolate into each half sphere mould and spread it out, making sure there is a thick enough layer (about 1–2mm) to coat the inside of the moulds. Allow to set at room temperature or in the fridge.
- Now place some parchment paper under the wire racks on which the biscuits are sitting. Pour half a tablespoon of chocolate over each cooled biscuit, covering them completely. Allow the excess chocolate to drip off, and then refrigerate to set.

MARSHMALLOW

1 large egg white
6g agar-agar (a natural, vegetarian setting agent available from Holland and Barrett or Whole Foods)
22ml cold water
83g granulated sugar
⅓ tablespoon golden syrup

Note Be careful when handling the sugar syrup as it will be very hot and will burn on contact.

- Tip the egg white into a medium or large bowl and set aside.
- Put the agar-agar into a small bowl and pour the water over it. Stir to dissolve.
- Pour the hydrated agar-agar into a small pan, then add the sugar and golden syrup and bring to the boil over a medium-high heat. When the syrup begins to boil, attach the sugar thermometer.
- When the syrup reaches 119°C, beat the egg white with an electric hand mixer until firm peaks form. Once the syrup reaches 121°C, slowly pour the syrup into the egg white in a thin stream, while beating continuously on a low speed. Once all the syrup has been incorporated, increase the speed to high and beat until thick and glossy. Keep beating until the bowl is cool to the touch.
- Spoon the cool marshmallow into the piping bag with the medium round tip (if using a disposable piping bag, cut a hole, about 5mm in diameter at the pointed end).

ASSEMBLE

filling of choice (such as raspberry or strawberry jam or caramel)
50g dark, milk or caramel chocolate, melted
sprinkles or chopped nuts, to decorate

- Pipe the marshmallow into the set chocolate moulds and top with your chosen filling, to come just up to the rim. Do not overfill.
- Spoon the melted chocolate into the piping bag with the small round tip (or, if using a disposable piping bag, cut a very small hole, about 2–3mm in diameter, at the pointed end).
- Pipe a ring of chocolate onto the base of each biscuit. Place a biscuit on top of each chocolate mould, with the piped edge touching the mould to 'glue' it together, then allow to set in the fridge.

- Once the chocolate is cold and has set, gently peel the teacakes from the silicone mould.
- To decorate the outside of the teacakes, pipe some melted chocolate round the edge of each teacake and then top this with sprinkles or nuts of your choice.

Variations

- Dark chocolate with a marshmallow and raspberry or strawberry jam centre.
- Dark or milk chocolate with a marshmallow centre and then covered with sprinkles.
- Milk chocolate filled with marshmallow, caramel and a whole hazelnut and sprinkled with chopped hazelnuts.
- Milk chocolate with a marshmallow and caramel centre.

VALENTINE'S DAY HEART BISCUITS

Valentine's Day is one of the busiest days of the year at Primrose Bakery and we always think of it as the start of spring, even though it's not strictly true. We have so much fun preparing and sending out themed cupcakes, cakes and biscuits and have even delivered a few marriage proposals on our cakes as well as witnessing some proposals at the bakery itself. But these biscuits most definitely do not have to be made only for Valentine's Day and are an opportunity to get creative with your decorating skills.

Makes about 12 large heart-shaped biscuits

EQUIPMENT

one large, heart-shaped cookie cutter
(about 12cm in diameter)
two piping bags with small round tips (or, if using disposable piping bags, you can cut a very small hole, about 2–3mm, at the pointed end)

HEART BISCUITS

85g unsalted butter
100g golden caster sugar
1 large egg
½ teaspoon vanilla extract
200g plain flour
½ teaspoon baking powder
¼ teaspoon salt

- Cream the butter and sugar together in a bowl, using an electric hand mixer, then add the egg and vanilla extract and mix until fully incorporated. Add the flour, baking powder and salt and mix until it all comes together. Wrap the dough in cling film and place in the fridge to rest for 20 minutes.
- Preheat the oven to 180°C/160°C (fan)/350°F/ gas mark 4. Lightly grease two baking trays and line with parchment paper.

- On a floured work surface, roll out the dough to about 5mm thick, then cut out about 12 heart shapes and place on the prepared baking trays, leaving a little space between each one to allow the biscuits to spread during baking.
- Bake for 10–12 minutes, until the biscuits are a light golden brown and firm to the touch. They will cook quickly, so keep an eye on the cooking time, and they will continue to cook a little once they are out of the oven.
- Transfer the biscuits to wire racks and leave to cool while you prepare the vanilla buttercream icing.

VANILLA BUTTERCREAM ICING

55g unsalted butter, softened
250g icing sugar
2 tablespoons milk
½ teaspoon vanilla extract
red and pink gel food colourings

- Put the butter, icing sugar, milk and vanilla extract into a medium bowl. Using an electric hand mixer on a low speed, mix together until all the ingredients are combined. Then beat for a further minute on a medium speed until the mixture is smooth and lump-free.
- Divide the icing between two bowls. Add the red food colouring to one bowl and the pink food colouring to the other, until you achieve the desired shades of pink and red. Transfer each different-coloured icing to separate piping bags.

ASSEMBLE

sugar decorations, sprinkles or sweets, to decorate

- When you are ready to ice the biscuits, lay them out on a flat work surface or tray. Pipe your desired name or message onto each heart and decorate with sugar decorations, sprinkles or sweets. If using sprinkles, pour them into a large, wide-rimmed bowl, covering the bottom of the bowl. Once you have piped your message, dip the iced heart straight into the sprinkles while the icing is still damp.

● One of the reasons the bakeries are painted in colours of pink, yellow and mint green is to try and bring as much summer and light as possible into the shops all year round. I love hot weather and try to be outdoors as much as I can although I do sometimes find the British summers a disappointment. Consequently, ever since Lisa and I opened the first bakery we have always tried to keep everything bright and cheerful. ● The best berries, and some other fruits, are available during the summer months and it's wonderful to be able to bake with all of them. We use plenty of strawberries and raspberries in our baking, and the cupcakes and cakes we make with them never fail to impress our customers. In this chapter, I have also included a couple of new cocktail cupcakes, based on popular summer drinks, as well as a few ideas for summer birthday cakes. ● With the lighter and longer days in summer, there are usually more opportunities for get-togethers, picnics and parties, so the addition of one of these cakes, cupcakes, loaves or slices would, I am sure, be very welcome.

ANGEL FOOD CAKE WITH BERRY AND MINT SALAD

This simple but delicious cake would make a lovely summer dessert
served with the fruit salad on the side, while the cake on its own is also good served
as a morning or afternoon snack with a cup of coffee or tea.

Makes one 25cm cake, serving 15–20

SPONGE

95g cake flour (a very pale, low-protein American
flour; if not available, use plain flour)
40g cornflour
8 large egg whites, at room temperature
1 teaspoon cream of tartar
½ teaspoon salt
250g granulated sugar
1 teaspoon vanilla extract

Note This recipe uses a two-piece aluminium
angel food cake tin (not non-stick) with cooling
feet. These are available to buy online, through
Amazon for example.

- Preheat the oven to 180°C/160°C (fan)/350°F/
  gas mark 4. Leave the cake tin ungreased.
- Sift the flour and cornflour together into a bowl
  and set aside.
- Place the egg whites in a large mixing bowl,
  add the cream of tartar and salt and then, using
  an electric hand mixer, beat on a medium speed
  until soft peaks form.
- Continue beating on a medium speed and add
  a quarter of the sugar at a time until all the
  sugar is used up. The mixture should be shiny
  and glossy. Add the vanilla extract and continue
  beating until stiff peaks form. Take care not to
  overmix, as overbeating the egg white and sugar
  will produce a dry and dull meringue mixture.
- Sift the flour mixture for a second time over this
  meringue mixture and, using a metal spoon or
  a rubber spatula, gently fold it in. Do not overmix
  or it will knock out all the air from the batter.

- Once all the ingredients are combined, pour the
  batter into the ungreased angel food cake tin
  and gently spread it out evenly.
- Bake for 20–25 minutes, until the top of the cake
  is a light golden brown and an inserted skewer
  comes out clean.
- Remove from the oven, then invert the tin over
  a raised wire rack and leave the cake to cool
  completely before removing from its tin.
- Once the cake is cool, run a knife around the
  edges and the centre tube of the tin. Then run
  the knife between the tin base and the cake and
  invert the cake onto a cake board or serving plate.

BERRY AND MINT SALAD

1 punnet strawberries, washed, hulled and cut
into quarters
1 punnet blueberries, washed
1 punnet raspberries, washed
1 punnet cherries (if available), washed and pitted
a handful of fresh mint leaves (about 10 leaves),
finely chopped
2 tablespoons granulated sugar

- Add all the ingredients to a large bowl and mix
  well to combine. Place in the fridge to allow
  the fruit to infuse while the cake is cooling.
- Serve a portion of fruit with a slice of cake
  per person.

APEROL SPRITZ CAKE

In the last few years, the Italian Aperol Spritz cocktail, which is made by mixing the orange flavoured aperitif Aperol with Prosecco and soda water, has become hugely popular. It is a refreshing early evening summer drink with its flavours of orange, vanilla and herbs and I wanted to try it as a cake. Our chef Mary made it for the first time on my birthday and I couldn't have asked for a better birthday cake.

Makes one 20cm two-layer cake, serving 10–12

ORANGE SPONGE

250g plain flour
3 teaspoons baking powder
½ teaspoon salt
300g golden caster sugar
115ml milk
135ml fresh orange juice
125ml vegetable oil
3 large eggs
2 teaspoons grated orange zest

- Preheat the oven to 180°C/160°C (fan)/350°F/gas mark 4. Grease two 20cm sandwich tins and line with parchment paper.
- Place the flour, baking powder, salt and sugar in a bowl. Stir to combine, then make a well in the centre.
- Pour the milk, orange juice, oil, eggs and zest into a separate bowl and mix together.
- Pour the wet mixture into the well of the dry mixture and mix together until smooth.
- Divide the batter evenly between the two sandwich tins.
- Bake for 20–25 minutes, or until the cakes are golden brown on top and an inserted skewer comes out clean. Allow the cakes to cool in their tins for 10 minutes, then turn out onto wire racks to cool completely.

APEROL SPRITZ SYRUP

3 tablespoons Aperol
2 tablespoons Prosecco

- Combine the Aperol and Prosecco in a small bowl.
- Using a pastry brush, lightly brush the syrup over each cooled cake, until all of the syrup is used up, then leave to soak into the sponge.

APEROL SPRITZ BUTTERCREAM ICING

130g unsalted butter
530g icing sugar
4 tablespoons Aperol
2 tablespoons Prosecco
zest of 1 orange

- Put all ingredients into a large bowl and, using an electric hand mixer, mix on a low speed until all the ingredients are combined. Scrape down the sides of the bowl, then mix for a further minute until the icing is smooth and fluffy.

ASSEMBLE

orange zest, to decorate (optional)

- Put one cake on a plate or cake board and spread a layer of icing over the top. Place the second cake on top.
- Ice the top of the whole cake with the remaining icing. Decorate if you wish, perhaps with a little more fresh orange zest, or simply leave plain.

BANANA SPLIT CAKE

This triple-layer cake would make an amazing centrepiece on any table.
You will need to allow a little more time than for some of the other cakes in this book
and also need to finish the cake at the last moment, just before
serving, but I think you will find it's well worth the extra time and effort.

Makes one 20cm triple-layer cake, serving 10–12

VANILLA SPONGE

115g unsalted butter
115g golden caster sugar
2 large eggs
105g self-raising flour
12g cornflour
½ teaspoon baking powder
1½ tablespoons milk
1 teaspoon vanilla extract

- Preheat the oven to 180°C/160°C (fan)/350°F/
  gas mark 4. Grease three 20cm sandwich tins
  and line with parchment paper.
- In a bowl, cream the butter and sugar together
  with an electric hand mixer, until light and
  fluffy. Add the eggs one at a time, making sure
  the first one is well incorporated before adding
  the second.
- Add the flour, cornflour and baking powder
  and mix until just combined. Add the milk
  and vanilla extract and mix again until just
  combined. Do not overmix or this will result
  in a denser cake.
- Pour the batter into one of the prepared
  sandwich tins and spread it out evenly. Put
  to one side while you make the strawberry
  sponge, right.

STRAWBERRY SPONGE

115g strawberries, washed and hulled
135g self-raising flour
¼ teaspoon baking powder
a pinch of salt
120g unsalted butter
95g golden caster sugar
1 large egg
¼ teaspoon pink gel food colouring

- Place the strawberries in a food processor
  bowl and blitz until smooth and puréed.
- Stir the flour, baking powder and salt together
  in a bowl and set aside.
- Cream the butter and sugar together in
  a separate bowl until light and fluffy. Add the
  egg and beat in. Add the flour mixture and mix
  on a low speed until combined.
- Pour the strawberry purée and the pink
  food colouring into the batter and beat until
  well combined.
- Pour the batter into the second sandwich tin
  and spread it out evenly.
- Bake both the vanilla and strawberry sponges
  for 25–30 minutes, or until the tops of the
  cakes are golden brown and an inserted skewer
  comes out clean.
- Allow to stand in their tins for 15 minutes
  before turning out onto wire racks to cool.
- Turn the oven up to 190°C/170°C (fan)/
  375°F/gas mark 5. Make the chocolate sponge
  layer, page 82.

CHOCOLATE SPONGE

70g dark chocolate (70% cocoa solids), broken into small pieces
50g unsalted butter
110g soft brown sugar
2 large eggs, separated
110g plain flour
½ teaspoon baking powder
½ teaspoon bicarbonate of soda
a pinch of salt
150ml milk, at room temperature
1 teaspoon vanilla extract

- Melt the chocolate into a microwaveable or heatproof bowl, either in the microwave in short bursts or over a pan of gently simmering water, being careful not to let it burn. Leave to cool slightly.
- In a separate bowl, cream the butter and sugar together with an electric hand mixer until pale and smooth.
- In another bowl and with clean beaters, beat the egg yolks for several minutes. Slowly add the egg yolks to the creamed butter and sugar and beat well.
- Next, add the melted chocolate to this mixture and beat well.
- Combine the flour, baking powder, bicarbonate of soda and salt in another bowl. Pour the milk into a jug and add the vanilla extract.
- Add a third of the flour mixture to the chocolate, butter and sugar and mix well until combined, then beat in a third of the milk and vanilla extract and mix until combined. Repeat until all the flour and milk mixtures have been incorporated.
- In a clean bowl and with clean beaters, whisk the egg whites until soft peaks start to form. Carefully fold the egg whites into the cake batter, using a metal spoon – do not beat or you will take all the air out of the cake.
- Pour the batter into the third sandwich tin and spread it out evenly.
- Bake for 25–30 minutes, until the cake is firm to the touch and an inserted skewer comes out clean.
- Leave the cake to cool in its tin for about 10 minutes before turning out onto a wire rack to cool completely.

CHOCOLATE FUDGE SAUCE

40g dark chocolate (70% cocoa solids), broken into small pieces
50g milk chocolate, broken into small pieces
130ml double cream
20g golden syrup

- Put the dark and milk chocolate pieces into a heatproof bowl and set aside.
- Pour the cream and golden syrup into a small pan and bring to the boil over a medium heat. Once it starts to boil, pour it over the chocolate pieces. Using a wooden spoon or a spatula, gently stir until the chocolate has melted and you have a smooth consistency. Leave to cool.

ASSEMBLE

450ml double cream
1 tablespoon icing sugar
3 ripe bananas
500ml ice cream of your choice, from a tub
8–10 red maraschino cherries or fresh cherries with stems
chopped roasted peanuts (optional)

- In a bowl, beat the cream and icing sugar together until medium-stiff peaks form. Slice the bananas into 5mm-thick pieces.
- Place the chocolate sponge on a serving plate or cake board and spread half of the cream mixture over the top, leaving a 2cm border. Carefully arrange a layer of bananas over the cream, then place the strawberry sponge on top. Spread all but 50ml of the remaining cream on the strawberry sponge, leaving a 2cm border, followed by a final layer of banana. Then gently place the vanilla sponge on top of the bananas.
- Spread the chocolate fudge sauce over the top of the cake, then scoop balls of ice cream out of the tub and onto the centre of the cake. Using the remaining 50ml of cream, spoon or pipe 8–10 small mounds of cream around the outer edge of the cake and top each mound with a cherry.
- Sprinkle with chopped peanuts, if using and serve immediately.

BREAKFAST CAKE

One of the things we love to eat for breakfast at Primrose Bakery is our homemade granola, which we serve with fresh fruit and some plain yoghurt. So here is the cake version! This would work really well both for breakfast or a weekend brunch.

Makes one 20cm two-layer cake, serving 10–12

BANANA YOGHURT CAKE

180g unsalted butter, at room temperature
115g soft light brown sugar
2 large eggs
1 large ripe banana (about 70g), mashed
190g wholemeal flour
1 teaspoon bicarbonate of soda
1 teaspoon baking powder
a pinch of salt
190g natural yoghurt
100g homemade or shop-bought granola (the recipe for our granola can be found in our second cookbook, *The Primrose Bakery Book*)

- Preheat the oven to 180°C/160°C (fan)/350°F/ gas mark 4. Grease two 20cm sandwich tins and line with parchment paper.
- Cream the butter and sugar together in a bowl with an electric hand mixer until light and fluffy. Add the eggs one at a time, making sure the first one is well incorporated before adding the second.
- Beat in the mashed banana until mixed through.
- Add the flour, bicarbonate of soda, baking powder and salt and mix until just combined.
- Pour in the yoghurt and gently fold it in with a spatula until it is thoroughly combined and the mixture is smooth.
- Divide the mixture evenly between the two prepared sandwich tins.

- Using two-thirds of the granola (save the remainder for decoration), sprinkle a 2cm ring around the inside edge of one tin on the top of the batter.
- Bake for 25–30 minutes or until the tops of the cakes are golden brown and an inserted skewer comes out clean.
- Allow the cakes to cool in their tins before turning out and assembling.

ASSEMBLE

natural yoghurt
assortment of fresh fruit (such as pears, plums, grapes, berries)
reserved granola (see above)

- Place the cake without the granola on a serving plate or cake board.
- Spread a thin layer of yoghurt over the top of the cake. Neatly arrange an assortment of sliced fresh fruit over the yoghurt. Spread more yoghurt on top of the fruit and sprinkle with the granola.
- Carefully place the second cake on top.
- This cake is best eaten on the day it is made. As it contains yoghurt and fresh fruit, any leftover cake should be kept in the fridge.

CAMPARI AND GRAPEFRUIT CUPCAKES

Campari is one of my favourite pre-dinner drinks and it reminds me of the many happy times I've spent in Italy during the summer. My daughters know how much I love it, so much so that when we got our new Chihuahua puppy in February 2014, they suggested we call him Campari – and so we did!

Makes 10 regular-sized cupcakes

GRAPEFRUIT SPONGE

125g plain flour
1½ teaspoons baking powder
¼ teaspoon salt
150g golden caster sugar
50ml milk
75ml fresh grapefruit juice
65ml vegetable oil
2 large eggs
1 teaspoon grated grapefruit zest

- Preheat the oven to 180°C/160°C (fan)/350°F/ gas mark 4. Line a 12-hole muffin tin with 10 muffin cases.
- Place the flour, baking powder, salt and sugar in a bowl. Stir to combine, then make a well in the centre.
- In a separate bowl, mix together the milk, grapefruit juice, oil, eggs and grapefruit zest.
- Pour the wet mixture into the well of the dry mixture and mix together until smooth.
- Spoon the batter evenly into the muffin cases, filling each case to about two-thirds full.
- Bake for 18–20 minutes, or until the tops of the cakes are golden brown and an inserted skewer comes out clean. Leave to cool in their tin for about 10 minutes before turning out onto a wire rack to cool completely.

CAMPARI SYRUP

15g granulated sugar
1 tablespoon water
2 teaspoons grapefruit juice
½ tablespoon Campari

- Heat the sugar and water in a small pan over a low to medium heat until the sugar has dissolved. Allow to cool for about 10 minutes, then add the grapefruit juice and Campari. Stir to combine, then set aside.

CAMPARI AND GRAPEFRUIT BUTTERCREAM ICING

65g unsalted butter, softened
265g icing sugar
1½ tablespoons Campari
1½ tablespoons fresh grapefruit juice
zest of ¼ grapefruit (optional)

- Place all the ingredients in a large bowl. Using an electric hand mixer, mix on a low speed until all the ingredients are combined. Scrape down the sides of the bowl and mix for a further minute until the icing is smooth and fluffy.

ASSEMBLE

curls of grapefruit peel, to decorate (optional)

- Use a skewer to poke holes in the top of each cupcake, then using a pastry brush, brush the cooled cakes with the Campari syrup until all the syrup is used up. Leave to soak in.
- Ice each cupcake with the Campari and grapefruit icing and decorate with curls of grapefruit peel if desired.

CHERRY COLA CUPCAKES

A classic retro flavour combination, this works very well as a cupcake flavour,
providing you can avoid eating too many of the cola bottle sweets
as you make them. Remember to make the Cherry Sherbet Buttercream Icing the day
before you plan to use it.

Makes 12 regular-sized cupcakes

CHERRY COLA CUPCAKES

235g self-raising flour
¼ teaspoon salt
90ml cola concentrate (such as Soda Stream)
40ml cherry juice
40ml milk
125g unsalted butter
115g golden caster sugar
2 large eggs
maraschino or cocktail cherry syrup, for brushing
on top

- Preheat the oven to 180°C/160°C (fan)/350°F/ gas mark 4. Line a 12-hole muffin/cupcake tin with muffin cases.
- Combine the flour and salt in a bowl. Pour the cola concentrate, cherry juice and milk into a small jug. Set these aside.
- Cream the butter and sugar together in a bowl until light and fluffy, using an electric hand mixer. Add the eggs one at a time, making sure the first one is well incorporated before adding the second.
- Add half the flour mixture and mix until just combined. Scrape down the sides of the bowl, then add half the liquid mixture and mix until smooth. Repeat until all the flour and cola mixtures have been used up.
- Divide the mixture evenly between the muffin cases, filling each case to about two-thirds full.
- Bake for 18–20 minutes, or until the cakes spring back to the touch and an inserted skewer comes out clean.
- Allow the cupcakes to stand in their tin for 10 minutes before lightly brushing with the maraschino cherry syrup. Leave to stand for another 5 minutes before brushing with more syrup. Then allow to cool completely before icing and decorating.

CHERRY SHERBET BUTTERCREAM ICING

Make this icing the day before you plan to use it.

FOR THE SHERBET
1½ tablespoons citric acid (food grade)
½ tablespoon bicarbonate of soda
6 tablespoons icing sugar

FOR THE ICING
75g unsalted butter, softened
50g sherbet (see above)
500g icing sugar
75ml cherry juice

- Mix together the ingredients for the sherbet in a small bowl.
- To make the icing, put the butter, sherbet, icing sugar and cherry juice into a bowl. Using an electric hand mixer on a low speed, beat until all the ingredients are combined. Scrape down the sides of the bowl, then continue mixing for a further 45–60 seconds until the mixture is smooth and lump-free.
- Cover with cling film and allow to stand overnight or for at least 8 hours. Make sure there is enough space left in the bowl for the icing to rise (this is due to the reaction between the baking soda and citric acid).
- Once the icing is ready to use, mix it with a spatula until it is smooth and no air bubbles remain.

ASSEMBLE

fizzy cola bottle or sour cherry sweets, to decorate

- Ice each cupcake with the cherry sherbet icing and top with fizzy cola bottle or sour cherry sweets.

ICE CREAM CUPCAKES

A simple variation of our classic vanilla cupcakes, these would make
a welcome treat on a hot summer's day. You need
to make and eat them quickly though, before the ice cream melts!

Makes 12 regular-sized cupcakes

SPONGE

110g unsalted butter
225g golden caster sugar
2 large eggs
150g self-raising flour
125g plain flour
120ml semi-skimmed milk, at room temperature
1 teaspoon vanilla extract

- Preheat the oven to 180°C/160°C (fan)/350°F/
  gas mark 4. Line a 12-hole muffin tin with
  12 muffin cases.
- In a large mixing bowl, cream together the
  butter and sugar until the mixture is pale
  and smooth, which should take 3–5 minutes
  with an electric hand mixer. Add the eggs
  one at a time, making sure the first one is
  well incorporated before adding the second.
- Combine the two flours in a separate
  bowl. Pour the milk into a jug and stir in the
  vanilla extract.
- Add a third of the flours to the creamed butter
  and sugar and beat well. Pour in a third of the
  milk and vanilla extract and beat again. Repeat
  until all the flour and milk has been added.
- Carefully spoon the mixture into the muffin
  cases, filling each one to about two-thirds full.
- Bake for 20–25 minutes, or until the cakes
  have risen slightly and are golden brown
  on top. Allow to cool completely before icing
  and decorating.

ASSEMBLE

500ml good-quality vanilla or chocolate ice cream
sprinkles or sweets, to decorate

- Once the cakes have cooled, cut out a 2.5cm
  circle from the centre of each cupcake and
  either eat or discard.
- Remove the ice cream from the freezer and,
  if it is hard, place in the microwave for a few
  seconds. Pour the ice cream into a chilled
  mixing bowl.
- Using an electric hand mixer, beat the ice
  cream on a low speed until smooth.
- Working quickly, spoon a heaped tablespoon
  of ice cream on top of each cupcake, making
  sure you fill the centre of each cake.
- Decorate with sprinkles or sweets as desired
  and serve immediately.

LEMON TART

This fresh summer dessert is best made the day before you plan to eat it and
is lovely served with fresh cream or vanilla ice cream.

Makes one 20cm tart, serving 10–12

BISCUIT BASE

150g Rich Tea or digestive biscuits
zest of 1 lemon
60g unsalted butter, melted
50g desiccated coconut
2 egg whites (reserve 1 egg yolk for the filling)

- Preheat the oven to 180°C/160°C (fan)/350°F/
gas mark 4. Lightly grease a 20cm fluted tart
tin with a removable base.
- Put the biscuits into a food processor bowl and
blitz until they resemble fine breadcrumbs.
Alternatively, place the biscuits in a clip-seal
bag, remove the excess air and crush with
a rolling pin.
- Pour the crumbs into a bowl and add the rest
of the ingredients. Mix until all the ingredients
are well incorporated.
- Pour this mixture into the prepared tart tin and
press it down into the base and up the sides,
making sure it is evenly spread.
- Bake for 15–20 minutes until golden brown.
- Remove from the oven and allow to cool
while you prepare the filling. Turn the oven
down to 150°C/130°C (fan)/300°F/gas mark 2.

LEMON CUSTARD FILLING

3 large eggs
1 egg yolk
150g golden caster sugar
95ml double cream
zest of 1 lemon
85ml fresh lemon juice

- Place the pre-baked biscuit base on a baking
tray and set aside.
- Put all the ingredients except the lemon juice
into a large bowl and whisk together until well
incorporated. Now slowly add the lemon juice,
whisking well as you do so. Allow to stand for
15 minutes.
- Pass this mixture through a sieve into a jug,
then pour it over the biscuit base.
- Bake for 30 minutes until the sides are set, but
the middle is still slightly wobbly.
- Allow the tart to cool completely in its tin
before placing it in the fridge for at least
4 hours, or preferably overnight, to set further.
- Once the tart has cooled, carefully remove
from the tin, and serve.
- Any uneaten tart will keep in the fridge for
a couple of days.

NEAPOLITAN LOAF

The stripey Neapolitan ice cream, made up of layers of chocolate, vanilla and strawberry, inspired us to try these flavours as a loaf cake. When you cut into it, you'll find that the colourful layers make a pretty addition to the tea table.

Makes one 900g loaf, serving 8–10

LOAF

188g unsalted butter, at room temperature
188g golden caster sugar
4 large eggs
185g self-raising flour
15g cocoa powder
10ml milk
50g mascarpone cheese
60g strawberry jam
¼ teaspoon pink gel food colouring

- Preheat the oven to 180°C/160°C (fan)/350°F/ gas mark 4. Lightly grease a 900g loaf tin and line with parchment paper or a loaf tin liner.
- Put the butter, sugar, eggs and flour into a bowl and, using an electric hand mixer, beat on a low speed until all the ingredients come together.
- Divide this mixture evenly between three bowls.
- To the first bowl, add the cocoa powder and pour in the milk. Mix until well combined.
- To the second bowl, add the mascarpone cheese and mix until well combined.
- To the third bowl, add the jam and the pink food colouring and mix until well combined.
- Spoon a line of cocoa batter from the first bowl down the centre of the loaf tin, and even it out. Next, spoon a line of mascarpone batter from the second bowl directly on top of the cocoa layer. Then spoon a line of batter from the third bowl on top of the mascarpone. Repeat until all the batter is used up.
- Bake for 45–50 minutes, or until the loaf is golden brown on top and an inserted skewer comes out clean.
- Allow the loaf to stand in its tin for 10–15 minutes before turning out onto a wire rack to cool further.
- This loaf is at its best when eaten on the day it is baked, and even while it is still a little warm. If you do have some left over, wrap it in cling film and keep at room temperature for a day or two.

OMBRÉ LAYER CAKE

Along with our rainbow cake, this ombré cake has become one of the
most popular birthday cakes at our bakeries. As you cut into it,
the shades of pink look exceptionally pretty and I think you will find this
cake will go down well at any celebration.

Makes one 20cm five-layer cake, serving 12–15

SPONGE

335g golden caster sugar
315g self-raising flour
35g cornflour
1½ teaspoons baking powder
335g unsalted butter, at room temperature
6 large eggs
5 tablespoons skimmed milk
1½ teaspoons vanilla extract

GEL FOOD COLOURING QUANTITIES
Layer 1: ½ teaspoon pink plus ½ teaspoon red
Layer 2: 1 teaspoon pink
Layer 3: ½ teaspoon pink
Layer 4: ¼ teaspoon pink
Layer 5: ⅛ teaspoon pink

- Preheat the oven to 180°C/160°C (fan)/350°F/ gas mark 4. Grease five 20cm sandwich tins and line with parchment paper. (If you don't have five tins, you can bake the layers in batches.)
- Put the sugar, self-raising flour, cornflour and baking powder into a food processor bowl and pulse for 30–45 seconds, or until all the ingredients are well incorporated.
- Add the butter, eggs, milk and vanilla extract to the food processor bowl and blend for 5 seconds. Scrape down the sides of the bowl, then blend again for a further 4 seconds.
- Divide the batter equally between five bowls. Add a different colour to each bowl of batter in the quantities provided above.
- Pour each bowl of batter into a separate sandwich tin and spread it out evenly with a spatula.
- Bake for 12–15 minutes (you may need to do this in batches if you don't have enough oven space), or until an inserted skewer comes out clean.
- Transfer to wire racks and allow to cool. The cakes must be completely cool before the layers are assembled.

VANILLA BUTTERCREAM ICING

230g unsalted butter, at room temperature
120ml semi-skimmed milk
2 teaspoons vanilla extract
¼ teaspoon pink gel food colouring
1kg icing sugar

- Using an electric hand mixer, beat the butter, milk, vanilla, pink food colouring and half the icing sugar in a bowl until smooth. Gradually beat in the remainder of the icing sugar to produce an icing with a creamy, smooth consistency. Beat in more food colouring if you want a darker colour.
- The icing can be stored in an airtight container for up to 3 days at room temperature. Beat well again before reusing.

ASSEMBLE

pink sprinkles, to decorate

- Peel the parchment paper off all five layers of cake and if any of the cakes are domed, trim the tops to ensure they are as flat as possible before stacking.
- Place a small dollop of icing on the middle of a cake board or serving plate (this will act as 'glue' to help keep the cake stable as you build up the layers) and place the first cake on top. You can decide whether you prefer the layers to go from light to dark shades, or the other way round; just make sure you have them in one order of shading or another, not all jumbled up.
- Spread a thin layer of vanilla icing on top of the first cake, leaving a 1cm border. Then carefully place the second cake on top. Continue like this until all five cakes are stacked on top of each other, making sure you have enough icing left over to cover the top and the sides of the cake later.
- Place the whole cake in the fridge for 15–20 minutes to allow the icing to set.
- When the icing has set, crumb-coat the cake by spreading a thin layer of icing down the sides and on the top of the cake. This will ensure no crumbs fall away from the cake when you come to add a final layer of icing.
- Place the cake in the fridge for another 30 minutes, or until the icing is chilled and firm to the touch. Once it has set, spread the remaining icing around the sides and on the top of the cake to hide the colours of the layers.
- Decorate with pink sprinkles or in whatever way you like.

PASSIONFRUIT MELTING MOMENTS

Melting moment biscuits, with their shortbread texture and custard-cream-like filling, have been one of our bestsellers ever since we started the bakery. For this adaptation, we have substituted our usual filling with a passionfruit version, to make the perfect summer biscuit.

Makes 8 sandwich biscuits

BISCUITS

125g plain flour
125g cornflour
½ teaspoon baking powder
75g icing sugar
200g unsalted butter, at room temperature

- Place all the ingredients in a bowl and mix with an electric hand mixer until just combined. Wrap the dough in cling film and place in the fridge to rest for 20 minutes.
- Preheat the oven to 180°C/160°C (fan)/350°F/ gas mark 4. Line two baking trays with parchment paper.
- Roll 1 tablespoon of dough into a ball in your hand, and repeat until all the dough is used up. You should get about 16 balls. (Make sure you have an even number.) Place on the lined baking trays, leaving about a 5cm gap between each ball, as the biscuits will spread during baking. Gently press down the top of each ball with a fork to flatten it.
- Bake for 9–10 minutes, until the biscuits are firm to the touch and a light golden brown around the edges. Be careful not to overbake or they will become too crispy and dry. Leave to cool while you make the filling.

PASSIONFRUIT FILLING

95g unsalted butter, softened
215g icing sugar
35g fresh or tinned passionfruit pulp (fresh is better)

- Using an electric hand mixer, mix all the ingredients together in a bowl until smooth.

ASSEMBLE

icing sugar, for dusting

- Using an icing spatula or flat-edged knife, spread a small amount of the passionfruit filling on the flat side of 8 of the biscuits. Sandwich together with the remaining biscuits. Dust with icing sugar to finish.

PEACH BROWN-SUGAR SLICE

This slice would make a great summer snack or dessert. I'd recommend you use good-quality, medium-sized ripe peaches so you get the full benefit of their flavour, which really comes out during baking and is heightened by the rich, caramelised brown sugar.

Makes one 33×23cm tray, serving 15

BASE

5–6 medium-sized ripe peaches
435g self-raising flour
¾ teaspoon bicarbonate of soda
¼ teaspoon salt
260g unsalted butter, at room temperature
165g soft light brown sugar
135g dark brown sugar
3 large eggs
1½ teaspoons vanilla extract
170ml milk
double cream or crème fraîche, to serve (optional)

- Preheat the oven to 180°C/160°C (fan)/350°F/ gas mark 4. Lightly grease the base and sides of a 33 × 23cm baking tray and line with parchment paper. Leave a little overhang of paper, which will allow for easy removal of the slice later.
- Wash and halve the peaches and remove their stones. Cut a circle about 5mm thick from the ciut side of each peach half, and set aside.
- Combine the flour, bicarbonate of soda and salt in a bowl and set aside.
- In a separate bowl, cream the butter and sugars together with an electric hand mixer until light and fluffy. Add the eggs one at a time, making sure each one is well incorporated before adding the next. Add the vanilla extract with the last egg. Add the flour mixture and beat on a low speed until the mixture just comes together, then pour in the milk and mix until the batter is smooth.

- Pour this batter into the prepared baking tray and spread it out evenly across the base with a spatula. Arrange the rings of peach neatly on the surface of the batter.
- Bake for 30–40 minutes, until the slice is golden brown and an inserted skewer comes out clean.
- Allow the slice to stand in its tray for 15–20 minutes before removing to a wire rack to cool. (Simply remove it from the tray by holding the edges of the parchment paper to lift the whole slice out.)

GLAZE

2 tablespoons peach or apricot jam
2 teaspoons water

- Put the jam and water into a small pan and bring to a simmer over a medium heat. Allow to simmer for 1 minute, then remove from the heat and brush the glaze over the top of the peach slice.
- Cut the slice into portions and serve with whipped cream or crème fraîche if desired.

PEACH MELBA CAKE

Peach melba, made up of peaches, raspberry sauce and vanilla ice cream, is a very summery dessert which dates back to the 1890s when it was invented at the Savoy Hotel in London. At the end of this recipe you will find a variation for peach melba cupcakes, should you prefer these to a whole cake.

Makes one 20cm two-layer cake, serving 10–12

PEACH COMPOTE

7 ripe peaches
150g granulated sugar
150ml water
2 teaspoons vanilla extract

- Wash and peel the peaches, then cut in half and remove the stones. Cut the flesh into cubes and set aside.
- Put the sugar, water and vanilla extract into a medium or large pan over a medium-high heat and bring to a simmer.
- Carefully add the diced peaches and allow to simmer on a medium heat for 10 minutes, or until the peaches are soft.
- Remove from the heat and roughly mash the peaches with a fork. Set aside to cool completely. (You will be using half the compote to fold into the peach sponge, below, and the remaining half to spread in the middle of the layer cake.)

PEACH SPONGE

240ml semi-skimmed milk, at room temperature
6 large egg whites, at room temperature
1 teaspoon vanilla extract
290g plain flour
25g cornflour
4 teaspoons baking powder
½ teaspoon salt
360g golden caster sugar
170g unsalted butter, softened
½ quantity cooled Peach Compote (see left)

- Preheat the oven to 180°C/160°C (fan)/350°F/gas mark 4. Grease two 20cm sandwich tins and line with parchment paper.
- Put the milk, egg whites and vanilla extract into a bowl and mix together gently with a fork.
- In a separate bowl, combine the plain flour, cornflour, baking powder, salt and sugar. Add the softened butter and, using an electric hand mixer, mix until all the ingredients are just combined and the mixture resembles breadcrumbs.
- Pour in half the milk and vanilla mixture and mix on a low speed until all the ingredients start to come together. Add the remaining milk mixture and beat until smooth. Do not overmix this batter.
- Using a spatula, gently fold in the cooled peach compote until mixed through.
- Divide the batter between the two prepared sandwich tins. Bake for 25–30 minutes, until the cakes are golden brown on top and an inserted skewer comes out clean.
- Allow the cakes to cool in their tins for 10 minutes, then turn out onto a wire rack and leave to cool to room temperature before assembling.

RASPBERRY COMPOTE

155g fresh raspberries
50g granulated sugar
juice of ½ lemon
1 teaspoon vanilla extract

- Place all the ingredients in a small pan over a medium heat and bring to a simmer. Allow the mixture to simmer on the medium heat for 3 minutes, or until the raspberries become soft and break down.
- Take the pan off the heat and allow to cool completely before using.

RASPBERRY BUTTERCREAM ICING

100g unsalted butter, softened
120g Raspberry Compote (see above)
450g icing sugar

- Place all the ingredients in a bowl and, using an electric hand mixer, beat on a low speed until all the ingredients are combined. Increase to a medium speed and continue beating for a further 30–45 seconds until the mixture is smooth.

ASSEMBLE

½ quantity Peach Compote (see page 111)
1 ripe peach, thinly sliced, plus 12 fresh raspberries, to decorate

- Place one cake on a serving plate or cake board. Spread the cooled peach compote on top of the cake, leaving a border of at least 1cm. Place the second cake on top.
- Ice the top of the cake with the raspberry icing and decorate with fresh peach slices and raspberries.

Variation
Makes 20 regular-sized cupcakes

PEACH MELBA CUPCAKES

- Follow the recipe, but instead of using two sandwich tins, line two 12-hole muffin tins with 20 muffin cases. Spoon the batter evenly into the muffin cases, filling each case to about two-thirds full.
- Bake in the oven for 20–25 minutes. Allow to cool completely on a wire rack.
- When the cakes are cool, gently cut a 2cm round from the centre of each cupcake, using a cupcake corer or small paring knife. Spoon the peach compote into the centre of each cupcake.
- Ice each cupcake with the raspberry icing. Decorate with fresh peach slices and raspberries.

PINEAPPLE
UPSIDE-DOWN SLICE

I have always loved upside-down cake, with its fruit and caramel-like texture and pretty appearance, and it works well as a slice, as we have done here.

Makes one 33×23cm tray, serving 15

BASE

12 tinned pineapple slices, drained (reserve the juice)
150ml pineapple juice (from above tins)
200g light brown sugar

- Lightly grease a 33 × 23cm baking tray and line with parchment paper.
- Drain the pineapple slices and reserve the juice from the tins.
- Measure out 150ml of pineapple juice and pour into a small pan, then stir in the brown sugar. Bring to the boil, then turn down the heat and allow the mixture to simmer until it takes on a thick syrup-like consistency. This will take about 3–5 minutes.
- Pour the syrup into the prepared tray, making sure it covers the bottom of the tray. Arrange the pineapple slices neatly in the syrup. Set aside while you prepare the sponge.

SPONGE

150g self-raising flour
1 teaspoon baking powder
150g unsalted butter, at room temperature
150g light brown sugar
3 large eggs
60ml sour cream

- Preheat the oven to 180°C/160°C (fan)/350°F/gas mark 4. Combine the flour and baking powder in a bowl and set aside.
- In a separate bowl, cream the butter and sugar with an electric hand mixer until light and fluffy. Add the eggs one at a time, making sure each one is well incorporated before adding the next. Add the flour mixture and mix until combined.
- Finally, add the sour cream and beat until thoroughly incorporated.
- Spoon the batter directly on top of the pineapple slices in the baking tray and spread it out evenly.
- Bake for 30–35 minutes, or until golden brown on top and an inserted skewer comes out clean.
- Allow to cool in the baking tray, then turn out onto a serving plate, pineapple-side-up, and peel off the parchment paper. Cut the slice into squares, or as desired. It might be nice to make the squares roughly the same size as the pineapple rings so you have a pineapple ring in the middle of each square.

RAINBOW CUPCAKES

Here we have turned our rainbow layer cake into cupcake form. Once the cupcakes are covered with their cream-coloured icing, no one will know what lies underneath, so these would make a nice surprise for children when they cut or bite into them and all the colours are revealed.

Makes 12 regular-sized cupcakes

RAINBOW SPONGE

160g self-raising flour
1 teaspoon baking powder
15g cornflour
170g unsalted butter, at room temperature
170g golden caster sugar
3 large eggs
1 teaspoon vanilla extract
3 tablespoons milk
approx. ⅛ teaspoon each red, green, yellow, blue and pink gel food colourings

- Preheat the oven to 180°C/160°C (fan)/350°F/ gas mark 4. Line a 12-hole muffin tin with 12 muffin cases.
- Stir the flour, baking powder and cornflour together in a bowl, then set aside.
- In a separate bowl, cream together the butter and sugar with an electric hand mixer until pale and fluffy. Add the eggs one at a time, making sure each one is well incorporated before adding the next. Add the vanilla extract with the last egg. Add the flour mixture and mix until just combined, then pour in the milk and beat until mixed through.
- Divide the batter between five bowls and add a different food colouring to each bowl.
- Spoon a heaped teaspoon each of the different coloured batters into each muffin case, filling them to about two-thirds full. Then, using a skewer, lightly swirl the batter in each case to mix the colours. Be careful not to overmix.

- Bake for 20–25 minutes, or until an inserted skewer comes out clean.
- Allow the cakes to stand in their tin for 10 minutes before transferring to a wire rack to cool.

VANILLA BUTTERCREAM ICING

115g unsalted butter, at room temperature
60ml semi-skimmed milk
1 teaspoon vanilla extract
500g icing sugar

- Using an electric hand mixer, beat the butter, milk, vanilla extract and half the icing sugar in a bowl until smooth. Gradually beat in the remaining icing sugar, to produce an icing with a creamy, smooth consistency.

ASSEMBLE

multi-coloured sprinkles, to decorate

- Ice each cupcake with the vanilla icing and decorate with colourful sprinkles.

STRAWBERRY BASIL CAKE

Strawberries and sponge go very well together, and this moist fruity cake would make a lovely summer treat when strawberries are in abundance. The basil and vinegar add a slightly different and unique taste, but I hope you will agree that this is only a good thing.

Makes one 20cm two-layer cake, serving 10–12

MACERATED STRAWBERRIES

230g fresh strawberries, washed and hulled
8 basil leaves, large
1 teaspoon balsamic vinegar
1 tablespoon golden caster sugar

- Dice the strawberries and place in a bowl. Slice the basil leaves thinly and add to the strawberries. Add the vinegar and sugar and stir through until all the ingredients are well combined. Allow the strawberries to stand for 30 minutes to macerate.

STRAWBERRY SPONGE

265g self-raising flour
½ teaspoon baking powder
¼ teaspoon salt
240g unsalted butter, at room temperature
190g golden caster sugar
2 large eggs
Macerated Strawberries (see left)

- Preheat the oven to 180°C/160°C (fan)/350°F/ gas mark 4. Grease two 20cm sandwich tins and line with parchment paper.
- Combine the flour, baking powder and salt in a bowl and set aside.
- In a separate bowl, cream the butter and sugar together with an electric hand mixer until light and fluffy. Add the eggs one at a time, making sure the first one is well incorporated before adding the second. Add the flour mixture and mix on a low speed until combined. Pour in the macerated strawberries and fold through with a spatula.
- Divide the batter between the two sandwich tins, spreading it out evenly.
- Bake for 25–30 minutes, or until the cakes are golden brown on top and an inserted skewer comes out clean.
- Allow the cakes to stand in their tins for 15 minutes before turning out onto wire racks to cool completely.

STRAWBERRY SYRUP

160g strawberries, washed and hulled
1 tablespoon golden caster sugar

- Roughly chop the strawberries and place in a small pan along with the sugar. Place over a low heat for 15–20 minutes, stirring regularly and mashing the strawberries with a fork until they break down and a thick jam-like syrup forms. Allow to cool completely before using in the icing.

STRAWBERRY ICING

125g unsalted butter, softened
80g cream cheese, softened
85g Strawberry Syrup (see left)
470g icing sugar

- Put all the ingredients into a bowl and, using an electric hand mixer, beat on a low speed until all the ingredients come together. Scrape down the sides of the bowl, then beat on a medium speed until the icing is smooth. Do not overmix.

ASSEMBLE

fresh strawberries, to decorate (optional)
3–4 fresh basil leaves (optional)

- Place one cake on a cake board or serving plate. Spread a layer of strawberry icing over the top the cake, then carefully place the second cake on top. Spread the remaining icing around the sides and the top of the whole cake. Decorate with fresh strawberries if you wish and perhaps a few leaves of fresh basil.
- This cake will be at its best if eaten on the day it is made.

STRAWBERRY MILKSHAKE CAKE

A fun, summery cake that would appeal particularly to children, but which,
in our kitchens, has also proved popular with adults who like
the distinctive taste of the Nesquik milkshake powder in the icing!

Makes one 20cm triple-layer cake, serving 10–12

STRAWBERRY MILKSHAKE CAKE

390g plain flour
1 tablespoon baking powder
½ teaspoon salt
250g unsalted butter
450g granulated sugar
7 large egg whites
115g yoghurt
115ml milk

- Preheat the oven to 180°C/160°C (fan)/350°F/ gas mark 4. Grease three 20cm sandwich cake tins and line with parchment paper.
- Combine the flour, baking powder and salt in a bowl, then set aside.
- In a separate bowl, cream the butter and sugar together with an electric hand mixer until light and fluffy.
- In another bowl, mix together the egg whites, yoghurt and milk.
- Pour half of the flour mixture and half of the yoghurt and milk mixture into the creamed butter and sugar and beat until the mixture just starts to come together. Add the remaining flour and yoghurt and milk mixtures and beat until thoroughly combined.
- Divide the batter between the three sandwich tins.
- Bake for 20–25 minutes, until an inserted skewer comes out clean. Leave the cakes to cool in their tins for 10 minutes, then turn out onto wire racks to cool completely.

STRAWBERRY MILKSHAKE ICING

120g unsalted butter, at room temperature
600g icing sugar
30g cream cheese
3 tablespoons instant strawberry milkshake powder (such as Nesquik) dissolved in 4½ tablespoons milk

- Put all the ingredients into a bowl and beat together until you have a smooth icing.

ASSEMBLE

fresh strawberries to decorate (optional)

- If any of the cakes are domed, trim the tops to ensure the surfaces are as flat as possible before stacking.
- Place one of the cakes on a cake board or serving plate and spread some strawberry milkshake icing over the top. Carefully place the second cake on top and spread with another layer of icing. Repeat with the third cake and then ice the top of the whole cake. Decorate as desired, perhaps with some fresh strawberries.

TIFFIN SLICE

We recently made this for one of our staff parties, and to say it went down well is an understatement. It's one of those things that's hard to eat a just tiny bit of, and most people went back for a few helpings! This slice is simple to make and will keep well too, so you could make it in advance and serve when needed.

Makes one 33×23cm tray, serving 15

SLICE

400g malted milk biscuits
100g cocoa rice pops
60g desiccated coconut
85g dried apricots, roughly chopped
210g unsalted butter, cubed
100g milk chocolate
50g soft brown sugar
90g golden syrup
1 tablespoon cocoa powder
400g dark chocolate (70% cocoa solids), broken into small pieces
cocoa powder (optional)

- Lightly grease the base and sides of a 33 × 23cm baking tray and line with parchment paper.
- Place the biscuits in a large bowl and break them up into bite-sized pieces, either by hand or with the end of a rolling pin. Add the rice pops, coconut and dried apricots, then stir to combine and set aside.
- Put the butter, milk chocolate, sugar, golden syrup and cocoa powder into a pan over a low heat and heat gently, stirring frequently, until the chocolate has melted and the mixture is smooth.
- Pour this chocolate mixture over the biscuit mixture and stir together until well incorporated. Pour into the prepared tray and, using a spatula, spread it out evenly and gently press it down into the tray.
- Melt the dark chocolate in a microwaveable or heatproof bowl, either in the microwave in short bursts or over a pan of lightly simmering water. Once it has melted, pour it over the mixture in the tray and spread it out evenly with a palette knife so it covers the entire surface.
- Place the tray in the fridge for a minimum of 2–3 hours to set. Once it has set, sprinkle top with cocoa powder (optional), cut into squares and serve.

SUMMER VEGETABLE MUFFINS

We don't often make savoury things at our bakeries, but every once in a while
we all feel like something that's not too sweet, and these fresh,
seasonal muffins would be lovely served at a picnic or for afternoon tea.

Makes 15 regular-sized muffins

MIXED VEGETABLES

1½ tablespoons vegetable oil
¼ brown onion, diced
40g carrots, diced
2 cloves garlic, finely chopped
1 medium red pepper, diced
90g courgettes, grated
50g green peas
100g sweetcorn kernels
salt and pepper, to taste

- Heat the oil in a frying pan until it is hot but not smoking. Add the onion and carrot and fry over a medium heat until the onion starts to become transparent. Add the garlic and red pepper and continue cooking for a further minute, then add the remaining vegetables and cook for a further 2 minutes, or until the carrots are soft.
- Season with salt and pepper to taste, then remove from the heat and set aside to cool.

MUFFINS

350g self-raising flour
½ teaspoon salt
¼ teaspoon ground black pepper
½ teaspoon baking powder
100g unsalted butter
130ml milk
100ml vegetable oil
2 large eggs
1 batch Mixed Vegetables (see left)
50g grated cheddar cheese, for sprinkling on top

- Preheat the oven to 180°C/160°C (fan)/350°F/ gas mark 4. Line two 12-hole muffin tins with 15 muffin cases.
- Combine the flour, salt, black pepper and baking powder, then make a well in the centre.
- Melt the butter in a pan and pour in the milk and vegetable oil. Add the eggs and stir to combine.
- Add the butter mixture and mixed vegetables to the well in the flour mixture. Stir with a wooden spoon until all the ingredients come together. Do not overmix.
- Spoon the batter evenly into the muffin cases, filling them to about two-thirds full, and top each one with a sprinkling of grated cheddar cheese.
- Bake for about 25 minutes, until the tops of the muffins are a light golden brown and an inserted skewer comes out clean.
- These muffins would be best served warm, although any leftover muffins can be cooled and then stored in an airtight container for 2–3 days.

THREE-TIERED
SPRINKLE CONFETTI CAKE

I would recommend making this spectacular cake for a special occasion and allow yourself plenty of time to complete it. It is extremely colourful and fun, so it would also be a great cake to make with children.

Makes one triple-layer cake (one 15cm cake, one 10cm cake and one regular-sized cupcake), serving 8–10

SPONGE

210g self-raising flour
25g cornflour
1 teaspoon baking powder
225g golden caster sugar
4 large eggs
225g unsalted butter, softened
4 tablespoons skimmed milk
1 teaspoon vanilla extract
2 tablespoons colourful sprinkles

- Preheat the oven to 180°C/160°C (fan)/350°F/ gas mark 4. Grease one 15cm and one 10cm cake tin and line with parchment paper. Place one muffin case in a muffin tin.
- Put the flour, cornflour, baking powder and sugar into the bowl of a food processor and blend for 30 seconds until thoroughly mixed.
- Add the eggs, softened butter, milk and vanilla extract and blend for 5 seconds, then scrape down the sides of the bowl and blend again for a further 5 seconds.
- Add the 2 tablespoons of sprinkles and gently fold through. Spoon the batter into the two cake tins and the muffin case, filling them to about two-thirds full.
- Place all the tins in the oven. Bake the cupcake for 12–15 minutes, the 10cm cake for 20–25 minutes, and the 15cm cake for 30–35 minutes, or until golden brown on top and an inserted skewer comes out clean.
- Allow to stand in their tins for 10–15 minutes before turning out onto wire racks to cool.

ASSEMBLE

Double batch Vanilla Icing (see recipe on page 116 and double the quantities)

100g each of 2 different types of colourful sprinkles (any shape), to decorate

- Start with the 15cm and 10cm cakes. If they are domed, trim the tops to ensure they have a flat surface before stacking. Place the cakes on separate plates and cover the sides and the top of each one with a thin layer of vanilla icing. Place the cakes in the fridge or freezer until the icing has set.
- When set, ice the tops and sides of both cakes with another layer of icing, making sure all the surfaces are as smooth as possible. Place back in the fridge or freezer until the icing has set.
- Pour one type of sprinkles into a bowl that is large enough to fit the 15cm cake but is not too deep. Place a piece of parchment paper (the size of the palm of your hand) on top of the 15cm cake and gently run a knife under the base of the cake. Remove the cake from the plate, then carefully roll the sides of the cake into the sprinkles, pressing down gently while rolling to ensure that the sprinkles stick. Then, holding the base of the cake with one hand, use the other hand to remove the parchment paper. Take small handfuls of the sprinkles and gently pat them on the top of the cake to cover the surface. Place the cake back on its serving plate and put a small dollop of icing on the middle of the cake.
- Repeat the above steps with the 10cm cake, using the second type of sprinkles, then carefully place it on top of the 15cm cake and press down gently to ensure the dollop of icing spreads out on the base and acts as the glue between the two cakes. If needed, carefully fill any gaps in the icing with more sprinkles.
- Ice the cupcake and sprinkle as desired, then stick it on top of the 10cm cake, using a small amount of icing on its base to attach it.

The biggest day in Primrose Bakery's autumn calendar is Halloween, and the trick-or-treaters often come into the shops, the cutest ones by far being the tiny children dressed as ghosts and witches. At this time of year we make lots of cakes containing pumpkin, apples and nuts and a hint of the more indulgent ingredients we all feel like eating when the days are getting shorter and a bit colder. There are several gluten-free options in this chapter too, all of which I think you will enjoy whether or not you follow a gluten-free diet. Our 'free from' range has grown considerably in the last couple of years as the demand for these items has increased, but we always try to maintain a very high quality and to make things that appeal to everyone, whatever their diet.

APPLE AND RAISIN
OATMEAL COOKIES

The perfect cookie to make for an autumn teatime treat or to enjoy with your morning coffee or tea. These cookies keep well in an airtight container for up to a week, so you can easily make a batch in advance and then have them ready for any occasion.

Makes 18 cookies

COOKIES

125g grated apple (approx. 1 large apple), using coarse side of grater
160g plain flour
1 teaspoon bicarbonate of soda
95g rolled oats
140g unsalted butter
75g soft light brown sugar
95g golden caster sugar
1 teaspoon vanilla extract
1 large egg
85g raisins

- Place the grated apple in a frying pan over a low heat and cook for 3–5 minutes, or until no moisture is left in the apples. You just want to dry the apples, so they should not take on any colour. Set aside and allow to cool slightly.
- Stir the flour, bicarbonate of soda and rolled oats together in a bowl, then set aside.
- In a separate bowl and using an electric hand mixer, cream the butter and sugars together until light and fluffy. Add the vanilla extract and the egg and mix until well combined. Add the flour mixture and mix until all the ingredients are just combined and the mixture starts to resemble a dough.
- Fold the slightly cooled apple and the raisins into the dough.
- Wrap the dough in cling film and place in the fridge to rest for 30 minutes.

- Preheat the oven to 180°C/160°C (fan)/350°F/ gas mark 4. Lightly grease two baking trays and line with parchment paper.
- The dough will be soft, so using two tablespoons, one to pick up some dough and the other to push it off onto the tray, place spoonfuls of dough on the trays, leaving a gap of at least 3cm between each one. Do not crowd the tray as the cookies will spread during cooking.
- Bake for 18–20 minutes, or until the cookies are golden brown.
- Allow to cool on their trays for 5 minutes before transferring to wire racks to cool completely.

BLACK SESAME CUPCAKES

Black sesame is found in many Asian cakes and other foods. Its distinctive aromatic flavour and dark colour make these cakes look and taste quite different from our usual style of cupcakes, but I think they are just as delicious.

Makes 15 regular-sized cupcakes

BLACK SESAME PASTE

155g black sesame seeds
40g golden caster sugar
80g honey
35ml water

- Place the black sesame seeds in a frying pan over a low heat and toast until they are aromatic (about 1–2 minutes), stirring frequently. Be careful not to let the seeds burn.
- Pour the toasted seeds straight into a food processor bowl and blitz until they resemble fine crumbs, scraping down the sides of the bowl regularly. Leave in the food processor bowl.
- Add the sugar and honey to the frying pan and, again over a low heat, allow the sugar to dissolve. Once the mixture starts to boil, pour it into the food processor bowl and switch it on again. While it is processing, pour in the water and allow it to mix until a thick paste forms (about 30–60 seconds). Set aside to cool while you prepare the sponge.

BLACK SESAME SPONGE

115g plain flour
130g self-raising flour
½ teaspoon baking powder
¼ teaspoon salt
180g unsalted butter
160g golden caster sugar
3 large eggs
190g Black Sesame Paste (see left)
80ml milk

- Preheat the oven to 180°C/160°C (fan)/350°F/ gas mark 4. Line two 12-hole muffin tins with 15 muffin cases.
- Combine the flours, baking powder and salt in a bowl and set aside.
- In a separate bowl and using an electric hand mixer, cream the butter and sugar together on a medium-high speed until light and fluffy.
- Add the eggs one at a time, making sure each one is well incorporated before adding the next. Add the sesame paste and beat until well combined.
- Add half the flour mixture and mix until just combined, then pour in half the milk and mix through. Repeat until all the flour mixture and milk is used up.
- Spoon the batter evenly into the muffin cases, filling each case to about two-thirds full. Bake for 18–20 minutes, or until the tops of the cakes are golden brown and an inserted skewer comes out clean.
- Allow to stand in their tins for 5 minutes before turning out onto wire racks to cool.

→

BLACK SESAME
BUTTERCREAM ICING

70g unsalted butter, at room temperature
45g Black Sesame Paste (see page 138)
500g icing sugar
60ml milk

- Beat the butter and sesame paste together in a bowl until smooth.
- Add the icing sugar and milk and beat on a low speed until all the ingredients are well combined. Scrape down the sides of the bowl, then beat for a further minute on a medium speed until smooth.
- Ice each cupcake with the black sesame icing and either leave plain or decorate as desired.

CARAMEL CHOCOLATE
NUT CLUSTERS

These rich caramel chocolates can be made in a variety of flavours,
and would be nice served after dinner. You will need a sugar
thermometer to help you achieve the perfect caramel, but this is straightforward
to use and should not put you off giving these a go.

Makes 24 clusters

CARAMEL

225g dark brown sugar
120g unsalted butter
200g tin sweetened condensed milk
120g golden syrup
55ml maple syrup
¼ teaspoon vanilla extract
½ teaspoon black treacle or (dark) molasses
a pinch of salt
a selection of dried fruit, nuts, chocolate, candy and
sprinkles, to decorate

Note Please be extremely careful when
boiling the caramel as it is very hot and can
cause severe burns.

- Cover a large baking tray with kitchen foil and
lightly grease with melted butter. Alternatively,
you can line the tray with a silicone mat.
- Put all the caramel ingredients into a medium,
heavy-bottomed pan over a low to medium
heat. Stir the contents with a wooden spoon
until all the sugar has dissolved. To test, rub
a little bit of the caramel between your fingers
to check for sugar crystals. Brush down the
sides of the pan with a pastry brush dipped
in cold water to dissolve any sugar crystals
that may have formed there.
- Attach a clip-on sugar thermometer to the pan
and cook the caramel at a rolling boil until it
reaches 114°C, stirring slowly and constantly
with a wooden spatula to prevent the caramel
from burning on the bottom of the pan.

Continue to occasionally brush the sides down
with a wet pastry brush. Once the thermometer
reads 114°C, immediately remove the pan
from the heat. Carefully pour the caramel into
a deep metal bowl and leave to cool.
- Once the caramel has cooled, spoon rounds
of caramel about 3–4cm in diameter onto the
prepared baking tray, leaving a little space
between each one. Place the tray in the freezer
for 20 minutes.
- Place your chosen decorations into separate,
deep soup or pasta bowls (see page 145 for our
suggested flavour combinations).
- After removing the caramel rounds from the
freezer, put a small quantity of your decorations
on top of them. Make sure you push them
in slightly to ensure they won't fall off during
dipping. Place the caramel rounds back in the
freezer until they are completely set.

CHOCOLATE COATING

700g milk chocolate, broken into small pieces
2½ tablespoons vegetable oil

- When you are ready to dip the caramel rounds, put the chocolate and oil into a microwaveable or heatproof bowl and melt the chocolate, either in the microwave in short bursts or over a pan of lightly simmering water on the hob, stirring regularly to ensure no lumps remain. Let it cool slightly before you start dipping. This mixture can be reheated if it becomes too thick for dipping.

DIPPING

- Line a baking tray with parchment paper.
- Dip the frozen caramel clusters, one at a time, into the melted chocolate, then remove with a fork and let the excess chocolate drip off. Place on the lined baking tray and sprinkle with more decorations if desired. Leave to sit on the tray until the chocolate has completely set. Once it has set, you can decorate the clusters again by drizzling more chocolate over them.

SUGGESTED FLAVOUR COMBINATIONS

FOR GROWN-UPS

Coffee Walnut: Chocolate espresso beans with toasted walnuts.

Amaretto Cherry: Mix 1–3 teaspoons of amaretto, or to taste, into the cooling caramel before you spoon out the rounds, then put some toasted almonds and dried cherries directly on the rounds.

Classic fruit and nut: Salted peanuts and raisins (or dried fruit of your choice).

FOR KIDS

M&M's: Well, M&M's of course!

Popping Jelly Beans: Place some jelly beans in the cooling caramel before you spoon out the rounds and then dip in the melted chocolate. Before the chocolate sets, sprinkle the top of the cluster with flavoured popping candy.

CHIFFON PUMPKIN GINGER PIE

This slightly alcoholic version of a pumpkin pie would make an alternative to the traditional pumpkin pie at Thanksgiving or could be served at any autumn dinner celebration, but as it contains fresh cream, it should be eaten on the day it is made.

Makes one 23cm pie, serving 12–15

GINGER CRUST

140g shop-bought ginger snap biscuits
130g pecans
80g soft light brown sugar
½ teaspoon salt
80g unsalted butter, melted

- Preheat the oven to 180°C/160°C (fan)/350°F/gas mark 4. Grease a deep 23cm pie tin and set aside.
- Add the ginger snaps, pecans, brown sugar and salt to the bowl of a food processor and blitz until the mixture resembles fine breadcrumbs.
- Pour in the melted butter and blitz until well incorporated. Press this mixture evenly into the bottom and up the sides of the prepared pie tin.
- Bake for 15 minutes, or until the crust is firm to the touch. Allow to cool at room temperature for 10–15 minutes and then chill in the fridge while you prepare the filling.

PUMPKIN FILLING

3½ sheets fine leaf gelatine
230ml milk
150g soft light brown sugar
4 large egg yolks
350g pumpkin purée (from a tin)
½ teaspoon ground cinnamon
½ teaspoon ground ginger
¼ teaspoon salt
2 tablespoons brandy or rum
165ml double cream

- Soak the gelatine in a bowl of chilled water while you prepare the rest of the filling.
- Place the milk, brown sugar, egg yolks, pumpkin purée, spices and salt in a pan over a medium heat and bring to the boil, whisking all the time. Once it starts to boil, turn the heat down to a simmer for 1 minute and continue whisking to prevent the eggs from curdling.
- Take the pan off the heat and transfer the mixture to a large bowl.
- Remove the gelatine from the water and squeeze to remove the excess water. Add it to the bowl along with the brandy or rum, and whisk through the mixture. Cover the bowl with cling film and set aside to cool.
- Once the mixture is cool, whip the double cream until it has a medium-stiff consistency. Pour a little of the pumpkin mixture into the cream and mix together with an electric hand mixer. Keep beating and slowly add the remaining pumpkin mixture, then pour into the cooled pie shell. Refrigerate until cold and set.

GINGER CREAM

240ml double cream
30g icing sugar
ginger syrup (from a jar of crystallised ginger), to taste

- Beat the double cream and icing sugar together until soft peaks form. Gently fold in the desired amount of ginger syrup. Spread the cream evenly over the pie and serve immediately.

CRÈME BRÛLÉE CAKE

Crème brûlée is one of my favourite desserts and, as any Primrose Bakery fan
will know, we often turn our favourite desserts, chocolates and drinks
into cake or cupcake form. This one is slightly trickier to do because the custard
is quite unstable to hold together in a cake, but I think if you serve it as soon
as possible after it is made, it will go down a treat.

Makes one 20cm single-layer cake, serving 10–12

SPONGE

290g self-raising flour
½ teaspoon salt
160g unsalted butter, at room temperature
170g golden caster sugar
2 large eggs
1 teaspoon vanilla extract
80ml milk

- Preheat the oven to 180°C/160°C (fan)/350°F/ gas mark 4. Grease a deep 20cm springform cake tin and line the base with parchment paper.
- Stir the flour and salt together in a bowl, then set aside.
- In a separate bowl and using an electric hand mixer, cream the butter and sugar together until light and fluffy.
- Add the eggs one at a time, making sure the first one is well incorporated before adding the second. Add the vanilla extract with the second egg.
- Add half the flour and mix until just combined, then pour in the milk and mix until it is incorporated. Add the remaining flour and beat until smooth.
- Pour the batter into the prepared tin and spread it out evenly with a spatula.
- Bake for 20–25 minutes, until the edges of the cake start to turn golden brown. The centre of the cake should be firm but not completely cooked (you will be finishing it off in the oven later) and there should be minimal colouring on the top of the cake.
- Remove from the oven and leave the cake in its tin while you prepare the vanilla custard. Turn the oven down to 150°C/130°C (fan)/ 300°F/gas mark 2.

VANILLA CUSTARD

240ml double cream
150ml milk
1 teaspoon vanilla extract
3 egg yolks
2 large eggs
100g golden caster sugar
a pinch of salt

- Pour the cream, milk and vanilla extract into a small pan over a low heat.
- Put the egg yolks, whole eggs, sugar and salt into a bowl. Using a hand whisk, combine all the ingredients until you have a smooth batter.
- Heat the cream mixture until it starts to 'smoke' and let off steam, then immediately remove from the heat.
- Pour the hot cream into the egg mixture in a slow and steady stream, whisking all the while, until it is well incorporated. Strain this mixture into a heatproof jug.

ASSEMBLE AND COOK

2–3 tablespoons granulated sugar, for the sugar crust

- Carefully wrap the base and sides of the hot cake tin in kitchen foil. This will ensure water does not seep into the cake when it is baked in the water bath. Place the wrapped cake tin in a deep roasting dish and pour in enough boiling water to reach halfway up the sides of the cake tin. Gently pour all the hot custard mixture around the sides of the par-baked cake. The cake will slowly absorb all the custard mixture.
- Bake in the oven for 35–40 minutes, or until the custard has set.
- Allow the cake to stand in its water bath for 5–10 minutes before removing from the roasting dish. Let the cake cool completely in its tin, then cover the tin with cling film and place in the fridge to chill for at least 4–5 hours, or preferably overnight.
- Once the cake has chilled, run a knife around the sides of the cake and remove it from the tin. You will need to be patient and careful when doing this as the cake is very delicate.
- Just before serving, sprinkle the granulated sugar on top of the cake. Then if you have a cook's blowtorch, hold the flame just above the sugar while moving it round and round until the entire surface is golden brown and caramelised. Serve immediately.
- This cake is best eaten immediately after the sugar crust has formed. The sugar crust will dissolve slowly if any leftovers are placed back in the fridge.

CHOCOLATE CHEESECAKE CUPCAKES

These moist, chocolatey cupcakes were an instant hit with our customers,
and they really do look and taste like cheesecake.
I hope they turn out to be as big a hit in your household too.

Makes 18 regular-sized cupcakes

CHEESECAKE FILLING

250g cream cheese, softened
2 large eggs
90g golden caster sugar
a pinch of salt
150g dark chocolate chips (70% cocoa solids)

- Put the cream cheese, eggs, sugar and salt into a bowl and, using an electric hand mixer, beat until well combined. Stir in the chocolate chips with a spatula, then cover the bowl with cling film and chill in the fridge until ready to use.

CHOCOLATE SPONGE

200g golden caster sugar
200g plain flour
30g cocoa powder
1 teaspoon bicarbonate of soda
½ teaspoon salt
220ml water, at room temperature
120ml vegetable oil
1 teaspoon apple cider vinegar
1 teaspoon vanilla extract

- Preheat the oven to 180°C/160°C (fan)/350°F/ gas mark 4. Line two 12-hole muffin tins with 18 muffin cases, and set aside.
- Pour the sugar into a bowl and add the flour, cocoa powder, bicarbonate of soda and salt. Stir to combine all the ingredients, then make a well in the centre.
- In a separate bowl, mix the water, oil, vinegar and vanilla. Pour this mixture into the dry ingredients. Then, using an electric hand mixer, beat on a low speed until all the ingredients are combined and there are no lumps. The batter will be thin.
- Spoon the chocolate batter evenly into the muffin cases, filling them to about two-thirds full, then add one tablespoon of the cheesecake filling to each case.
- Bake for 30–35 minutes, or until the cakes are firm to the touch and an inserted skewer comes out clean.
- Allow the cakes to cool in their tins for 10 minutes before turning out onto wire racks to cool completely.

→

CHEESECAKE ICING

75g unsalted butter, softened
190g cream cheese, softened
600g icing sugar
1 tablespoon vanilla extract
20g cocoa powder

- Put all the ingredients except the cocoa powder into a bowl and, using an electric hand mixer, beat on a low speed until they are all combined. Scrape down the sides of the bowl, then continue beating on a low speed for a further 30–45 seconds until the icing has a smooth consistency.
- Divide the icing between two bowls. Add the cocoa powder to the icing in one of the bowls and mix on a low speed until combined. Leave the other bowl of icing unflavoured.

ASSEMBLE

- Cover one half of each cooled cupcake with the plain cheesecake icing and the other half with the chocolate cheesecake icing. Using a palette knife, swirl the icings together to create a marbled effect.

ESPRESSO MARTINI CUPCAKES

The range of cocktail cupcakes we developed for our third book,
Primrose Bakery Celebrations, was so successful that we now sell a flavour of cocktail
cupcake every Friday in our shops. The espresso martini
flavour is a more recent creation, but seemed a natural addition to our range.

Makes 15 regular-sized cupcakes

ESPRESSO SPONGE

2 teaspoons espresso powder
50ml hot water
225g golden caster sugar
225g self-raising flour
25g cornflour
225g unsalted butter, softened
4 large eggs
45 shop-bought chocolate-coated coffee beans

- Preheat the oven to 180°C/160°C (fan)/350°F/
gas mark 4. Line two 12-hole muffin tins with
15 muffin cases and set aside.
- Put the espresso powder in a cup or small jug,
add the hot water and stir to dissolve. Set
aside to cool.
- Add the sugar, flour and cornflour to the
bowl of a food processor and pulse for
30 seconds or until the ingredients are well
combined. Add the butter, eggs and cup of
cooled coffee and process for 15–20 seconds,
then scrape down the sides of the bowl and
continue processing until all the ingredients
are thoroughly combined.
- Spoon the batter evenly into the muffin cases,
filling them to about two-thirds full. Drop three
chocolate coffee beans into each case.
- Bake for 15–20 minutes, until an inserted skewer
comes out clean.
- Leave the cakes to cool in their tins for
about 10 minutes, then transfer to wire racks
to cool completely.

VODKA SOAK

2 tablespoons espresso powder
4 tablespoons granulated sugar
4 tablespoons water
4 tablespoons vodka

- Put the espresso powder, sugar and water into
a small pan and bring to the boil on the hob.
Turn down the heat and leave to simmer until
the mixture has a thick syrupy consistency.
This will take about 1–2 minutes. Set aside and
leave to cool. When the syrup is cool, stir in
the vodka.
- Pierce each cooled cupcake several times with
a skewer, then brush with the vodka soak until
it is all used up.

KAHLÙA BUTTERCREAM ICING

130g unsalted butter, at room temperature
500g icing sugar
60ml Kahlùa liqueur
1 teaspoon vanilla extract

- Place all the ingredients in a large bowl. Using an electric hand mixer, beat on a low speed until all the ingredients are combined. Scrape down the sides of the bowl, then beat on a medium-high speed for a further 30–60 seconds until the icing is smooth.

DECORATE

a little espresso powder, for sprinkling on top

- Ice each soaked cupcake with the Kahlùa icing and top with a light sprinkling of espresso powder.

GLUTEN-FREE FIG, BLACKBERRY AND ALMOND TORTE

Both fresh figs and blackberries have a very short season when they are at their best and don't seem to be around in the supermarkets for long, so try to make this cake when they are. It is delicious whether or not you follow a gluten-free diet.

Makes one 25cm single-layer cake, serving 15

TORTE

3 tablespoons demerara sugar
6 large ripe figs, quartered
1 punnet blackberries
160g unsalted butter, at room temperature
150g golden caster sugar
3 large eggs
1 teaspoon vanilla extract
zest of ½ lemon
200g ground almonds
150g rice flour
½ teaspoon gluten-free baking powder
a pinch of salt
whipped cream, to serve (optional)

- Preheat the oven to 180°C/160°C (fan)/350°F/ gas mark 4. Grease the sides and base of a 25cm springform cake tin and line the base with parchment paper.
- Sprinkle the demerara sugar evenly over the whole base of the tin.
- Arrange all but one of the fig quarters in a circle around the base of the tin, then place the remaining piece in the middle. Arrange the blackberries around the middle fig, covering the empty space. Set aside.
- In a bowl, cream the butter and caster sugar together with an electric hand mixer until light and fluffy. Add the eggs one at a time, making sure each one is well incorporated before adding the next. Add the vanilla extract and lemon zest with the last egg.
- Fold in the ground almonds, rice flour, baking powder and salt until well combined.
- Pour the batter over the fruit in the tin and spread it out gently and evenly, making sure all the fruit is covered.
- Bake on the middle rack of the oven for 35–40 minutes, until the cake is golden brown on top, firm to the touch and an inserted skewer comes out clean.
- Allow the cake to cool slightly in its tin for 2–3 minutes, then invert it onto a wire rack to continue cooling. The fruit will now be visible on the surface of the cake.
- This cake is definitely best eaten on the day it's made, preferably while still a little warm with some whipped cream on the side.

GLUTEN-FREE SALTED CARAMEL CUPCAKES

As our salted caramel cupcakes are so popular in both our shops we thought
we should come up with a gluten-free version so that more people could enjoy them.
I think the end result is pretty similar in taste to the original cupcakes.

Makes 12 regular-sized cupcakes

SPONGE

115g brown rice flour
1½ teaspoons gluten-free baking powder
a pinch of salt
150g unsalted butter, at room temperature
135g golden caster sugar
3 large eggs
¾ teaspoon vanilla extract
20ml semi-skimmed milk
12 pieces caramel chocolate (such as Galaxy)

- Preheat the oven to 180°C/160°C (fan)/350°F/
  gas mark 4. Line a 12-hole muffin tin with
  12 muffin cases.
- Stir the rice flour, baking powder and salt
  together in a bowl, then set aside.
- In a separate bowl and using an electric hand
  mixer, cream the butter and sugar together
  until light and fluffy. Add the eggs one at a
  time, making sure each one is well incorporated
  before adding the next. Add the vanilla extract
  with the last egg. Add the rice flour mixture and
  mix until well combined. Pour in the milk and
  mix again until you have a smooth batter.
- Spoon the batter evenly into the muffin cases,
  filling them to about two-thirds full, then place
  one piece of caramel chocolate in each cupcake.
- Bake for 15–18 minutes, until the cakes are golden
  brown on top and an inserted skewer comes out
  clean. Allow to stand in their tin for 10 minutes
  before turning out onto wire racks to cool.

DECORATE

1 batch Salted Caramel Icing (see recipe on page 246)
1 tube Werther's Original sweets, crushed into small
pieces with a rolling pin
a pinch of fleur de sel or sea salt

- Ice each cupcake with the salted caramel icing
  and decorate with a few of the crushed sweets
  and a pinch of fleur de sel or sea salt.

HONEY ROASTED CASHEW COOKIES

Cashew nuts, with their distinctive sweet, almost buttery flavour, work fantastically well in both savoury and sweet dishes. Roasting these cashews in honey gives the cookies an even sweeter nutty taste and texture.

Makes 24 cookies

HONEY ROASTED CASHEWS

250g whole raw cashews
50ml honey
10g unsalted butter
25g golden caster sugar

- Preheat the oven to 180°C/160°C (fan)/350°F/gas mark 4. Lightly grease a baking tray and line with parchment paper.
- Tip the cashews onto the lined baking tray and set aside.
- Heat the honey, butter and sugar in a small pan over a low heat until the butter has melted. Then turn the heat up to medium and bring the mixture to the boil. Once it starts to boil, turn down the heat and allow to simmer for 2–3 minutes until the syrup is golden brown.
- Pour the syrup over the cashews on the tray and, using a wooden spoon, stir to coat them all with the syrup.
- Place in the oven for 15–20 minutes, carefully stirring the cashews in their tray every 10 minutes, until they are a light golden brown. While the cashews are in the oven, you can get on with making the cookie dough (see right).
- Remove the cashews from the oven and allow to cool on their tray. Leave the oven on for baking the cookies.

Note Any leftover cashews can be stored in an airtight container for 3–4 days.

COOKIES

270g plain flour
1 teaspoon bicarbonate of soda
½ teaspoon salt
140g unsalted butter, at room temperature
150g golden caster sugar
50g honey
1 large egg
1 teaspoon vanilla extract
250g Honey Roasted Cashews (see left)

- Lightly grease two baking trays and line with parchment paper.
- Stir the flour, bicarbonate of soda and salt together in a bowl, then set aside.
- In a separate bowl and using an electric hand mixer, cream the butter, sugar and honey together until light and fluffy. Add the egg and vanilla extract and beat until well combined. Then add the flour mixture and mix until combined.
- Wrap the dough in cling film and place in the fridge to rest for 15–20 minutes.
- Divide the dough into 24 even pieces, then roll into balls and place on the lined trays, leaving a gap of at least 5cm between each ball. Flatten each ball slightly, using a spatula or the back of a spoon, to make a disc about 5–6cm in diameter. Gently press some honey roasted cashews on top of each disc, covering the whole surface. Bake for 15–18 minutes, until the cookies are golden brown and the edges are firm to the touch.
- Allow to stand on their trays for 5 minutes before removing to wire racks to continue cooling.
- These cookies can be stored in an airtight container for up to a week.

NUTELLA COOKIES

Nutella has acquired many devoted followers since it first came on to the market in Italy in the 1960s, and this chocolate hazelnut spread is now popular the world over. These simple cookies are quite a recent addition to our range and our customers certainly seem to love them.

Makes 10 sandwich cookies

COOKIES

140g unsalted butter
140g soft brown sugar
140g Nutella, plus 10 teaspoons for the filling
185g plain flour
25g cocoa powder
1 large egg

- Preheat the oven to 180°C/160°C (fan)/350°F/ gas mark 4. Lightly grease a baking tray and line with parchment paper.
- In a bowl, cream the butter, sugar and the 140g of Nutella together until smooth, using an electric hand mixer. Beat in the flour and cocoa powder. Add the egg and beat again until a dough starts to form.
- Divide the dough into 20 even-sized pieces. Roll each piece into a ball, then flatten into a disc shape with the palm of your hand and place on the lined baking tray. Put 1 teaspoon of Nutella in the middle of the disc and cover with another disc. Then gently press down on the edges to ensure that it is completely sealed. Continue like this until all the discs have been used. Don't overcrowd the baking tray; leave enough space between each 'sandwich' to allow them to spread during baking.
- Bake for 12–15 minutes, or until the cookie sandwiches are firm around the edges and set in the middle.
- These cookies are best eaten while still slightly warm, perhaps with a glass of milk on the side. Any uneaten cookies can be stored in an airtight container for a few days.

PEANUT BUTTER AND
BANANA CUPCAKES

A classic flavour combination, these cupcakes were developed by my daughter Daisy.
They could be left undecorated or sprinkled with dried banana chips
or even Reese's peanut Butter Cups or Pieces, or one of my favourite chocolates,
M&M's peanut butter chocolate candies, all of which are available
in some UK supermarkets or online.

Makes 15 regular-sized cupcakes

BANANA SPONGE

250g plain flour
2 teaspoons baking powder
125g unsalted butter, at room temperature
250g golden caster sugar
2 large eggs
1 teaspoon vanilla extract
4 very ripe bananas (preferably turning black), mashed

- Preheat the oven to 180°C/160°C (fan)/350°F/ gas mark 4. Line two 12-hole muffin tins with 15 muffin cases.
- Put the flour and baking powder in a bowl and stir to combine. Set aside.
- In a separate bowl and using an electric mixer, cream the butter and sugar until pale and smooth. Add the eggs one at a time, mixing briefly after each addition. Add the vanilla extract and beat again briefly.
- Gradually add the flour mixture and beat again until well combined. Do the same with the mashed bananas.
- Spoon the mixture evenly into the muffin cases, filling each case to about two-thirds full.
- Bake for 25 minutes, or until an inserted skewer comes out clean.
- Leave the cakes to cool in their tins for 10 minutes, then turn out onto wire racks to cool completely before icing.

PEANUT BUTTER BUTTERCREAM ICING

115g unsalted butter, at room temperature
100g smooth peanut butter
60ml semi-skimmed milk
1 teaspoon vanilla extract
500g icing sugar

- Beat the butter, peanut butter, milk, vanilla extract and half the icing sugar in a bowl until smooth. This will take a few minutes with an electric hand mixer. Gradually beat in the rest of the icing sugar to produce an icing with a smooth and creamy consistency.
- Spread the icing over each cupcake and decorate as desired.
- Store any unused icing in an airtight container for up to 3 days. Beat well again before reusing.

PECAN PULL APART BREAD

This loaf would be lovely served at breakfast or mid-morning as it's not particularly sweet, and it is even more delicious when eaten slightly warm, simply 'pulling' pieces from it. At Primrose Bakery we tend to use a lot of pecans, and although these are native to Mexico and parts of the southern US, they are easily available in the UK. Our American chef, Mary, created the recipe for this bread and as soon as it was out of the oven we couldn't stop eating it.

Makes one 900g loaf, serving 8–10

BREAD

11g active dry yeast
60ml warm water
85ml semi-skimmed milk
45g unsalted butter, melted
1 teaspoon vanilla extract
395g plain flour
50g golden caster sugar
¾ teaspoon salt
2 large eggs

- Combine the yeast and warm water in a bowl. Set aside in a warm place for about 10–15 minutes, until it is bubbly.
- Pour the milk, melted butter and the vanilla extract into a separate bowl and set aside.
- Add the flour, sugar and salt to another bowl. Stir to combine, then make a well in the centre. Pour the yeast mixture into the well along with the eggs.
- Using the dough hook attachment on an electric mixer, mix the dough on a low speed while pouring in the milk mixture in a slow, steady stream until a soft dough forms. Continue mixing for 3 minutes.
- Pat your hands with flour and form the dough into a ball. Knead a little flour into the dough if it is sticky until a smooth ball forms.
- Cover the bowl with cling film and put in a warm place to allow the dough to double in size. This will take about 1 hour.

PECAN FILLING

100g roughly chopped pecans
150g soft light brown sugar
10g ground cinnamon
a pinch of salt

- Mix the pecans, brown sugar, cinnamon and salt together in a small bowl.

ASSEMBLE AND COOK

30g unsalted butter, melted

- Grease a 900g loaf tin.
- Once the dough has doubled in size, turn it out onto a floured work surface. Roll it out into a large, thin rectangle, about 30 × 60cm.
- Brush the dough with the melted butter and sprinkle with the pecan filling.
- With a long sharp knife, cut the dough into long strips about 8–10cm wide. Stack the strips on top of one another until you have one large stack.

- Cut this into six equal stacks about 10 × 10cm square. Place one square horizontally in the prepared loaf tin and push it towards the end of the tin so that it bulges up in the middle. Repeat with the remaining squares, pushing them against each other in a row, until you have filled the tin. Cover with a clean tea towel and leave in a warm place to rise for 30 minutes.
- Preheat the oven to 180°C/160°C (fan)/350°F/gas mark 4.
- When the dough has risen, bake for 35–45 minutes, or until the loaf is firm and golden brown.
- Turn the bread out onto a wire rack and leave to cool for 10 minutes while you prepare the glaze.

GLAZE

50g unsalted butter
100g soft light brown sugar
30g semi-skimmed milk

- Put all the ingredients into a microwaveable bowl and microwave on a high power for about 2 minutes, or until the mixture starts to bubble.
- Place the loaf back in its tin and drizzle the glaze over it. Leave to set in the loaf tin before serving.

PECAN SLICE

This pecan slice is a regular feature on the menu at both our bakeries and it's the perfect accompaniment to an afternoon cup of tea or coffee.

Makes one 33×23cm tray, serving 15

BASE

240g plain flour
90g icing sugar
155g unsalted butter, cut into cubes and softened

- Preheat the oven to 180°C/160°C (fan)/350°F/ gas mark 4. Lightly grease the base and sides of a 33 × 23cm baking tray and line with parchment paper.
- Put the flour and icing sugar into a bowl. Stir to combine, then make a well in the centre.
- Add the cubed butter to the well in the flour and mix with a fork or your fingertips until the mixture resembles breadcrumbs.
- Tip this mixture into the base of the prepared tray and, using the back of a spoon, press it down firmly to create an even base.
- Bake for 15–18 minutes, or until it starts to brown around the edges. Remove from the oven (leave the oven on) and set aside while you prepare the topping.

PECAN TOPPING

155g soft light brown sugar
165g unsalted butter
50ml double cream
210g honey
1 teaspoon vanilla extract
385g pecans, roughly chopped

- Put all the ingredients except the pecans into a heavy-bottomed pan over a medium heat and bring to the boil.
- Once the mixture starts to boil, add the chopped pecans and stir through until they are well coated. Immediately pour this mixture over the prepared base and place in the oven.
- Bake for 30–35 minutes, or until golden brown.
- Leave the slice to cool in its tray before cutting into squares.
- Store any leftovers in an airtight container for 3–4 days.

PRETZEL BOTTOM CHOCOLATE CUPCAKES

A crunchy cupcake that is both salty and sweet and with the surprise of a pretzel bottom once you've bitten through the sponge, these would be fun to make with children. They will dry out more quickly than some of the other cupcakes, so try to eat them on the same day, or the day after you make them.

Makes 12 regular-sized cupcakes

PRETZEL BASE

200g shop-bought salted pretzel snacks
1½ tablespoons soft light brown sugar
85g unsalted butter, softened

- Preheat the oven to 180°C/160°C (fan)/350°F/gas mark 4. Line a 12-hole muffin tin with 12 muffin cases, and set aside.
- Put the pretzels into a food processor bowl and blitz until they resemble coarse breadcrumbs. Alternatively you can put the pretzels in a clip-seal bag, then remove the excess air and crush with the end of a rolling pin. Transfer the crumbs to a mixing bowl.
- Add the brown sugar and softened butter to the bowl and mix until well combined.
- Spoon this mixture evenly into the muffin cases, then press it down into the base of each case with the back of a spoon.
- Bake for 7–10 minutes, or until golden brown on top.
- Remove from the oven (leave the oven on) and leave to cool while you prepare the chocolate sponge.

PRETZEL BUTTERCREAM ICING

130g shop-bought salted pretzel snacks
70g unsalted butter, at room temperature
40ml semi-skimmed milk
½ teaspoon vanilla extract
300g icing sugar

- Blitz the pretzels in a food processor bowl until they resemble coarse breadcrumbs. Alternatively, place the pretzels in a clip-seal bag, remove the excess air and bash them with the end of a rolling pin.
  Using an electric hand mixer, beat the butter, milk, vanilla extract and half the icing sugar in a bowl until smooth. This will take about 1 minute. Gradually mix in the remaining icing sugar to produce an icing with a smooth and creamy consistency, then fold in the pretzel crumbs until well combined.

CHOCOLATE SPONGE

115g dark chocolate (70% cocoa solids), broken into small pieces
85g unsalted butter, at room temperature
175g soft brown sugar
2 large eggs, separated
185g plain flour
¾ teaspoon baking powder
¾ teaspoon bicarbonate of soda
a pinch of salt
250ml semi-skimmed milk, at room temperature
1 teaspoon vanilla extract

- Melt the chocolate in a microwaveable or heatproof bowl, either in the microwave in short bursts or over a pan of lightly simmering water on the hob, being careful not to let the chocolate burn. Leave to cool slightly.
- In a separate bowl and using an electric hand mixer, cream the butter and sugar together until pale and smooth.
- In another bowl and with clean beaters, beat the egg yolks for several minutes. Slowly add the egg yolks to the creamed butter and sugar and beat well.
- Next, add the slightly cooled melted chocolate to this mixture and beat well.
- Add the flour, baking powder, bicarbonate of soda and salt to another bowl and stir to combine. Pour the milk into a jug and stir in the vanilla extract.
- Add a third of the flour mixture to the chocolate, butter and sugar, then add a third of the milk and vanilla, beating well after each addition. Repeat until all the flour and milk is used up.

- In a clean bowl and with clean beaters, whisk the egg whites until soft peaks start to form. Carefully fold the eggs whites into the batter with a metal spoon. Do not beat or you will take all the air out of the cake.
- Spoon the mixture evenly over the pretzel base in the muffin cases, filling each case to about two-thirds full.
- Bake for 18–20 minutes, until the cakes are firm to the touch and an inserted skewer comes out clean.
- Leave the cupcakes to cool in their tin for about 10 minutes before turning out onto a wire rack to cool completely before icing.

ASSEMBLE

whole pretzels or chocolate-dipped pretzels

- Ice each cupcake with the pretzel icing and top with either a whole pretzel or some chocolate-dipped pretzels.

SNICKERDOODLE COOKIES

Their amazing name doesn't give much away about these cookies, but they are a fairly simple, cinnamon- and vanilla-flavoured biscuit from the US, and very delicious.

Makes 12 cookies

CINNAMON SUGAR

100g golden caster sugar
1½ teaspoons ground cinnamon

- Combine the sugar and cinnamon in a bowl and set aside.

COOKIES

188g plain flour
1 teaspoon cream of tartar
½ teaspoon bicarbonate of soda
¼ teaspoon salt
100g unsalted butter, softened
150g golden granulated sugar
1 large egg
¼ teaspoon vanilla extract

- Preheat the oven to 180°C/160°C (fan)/350°F/gas mark 4. Lightly grease two baking trays and line with parchment paper.
- Put the flour, cream of tartar, bicarbonate of soda and salt into a bowl and mix together with a wooden spoon.
- In a separate bowl and using an electric hand mixer, beat together the butter, sugar, egg and vanilla extract until pale and fluffy, then add to the flour mixture and rub together gently with your fingertips. Do not overwork the dough.
- When all the ingredients are just combined, wrap the dough in cling film and place in the fridge to rest for at least 1 hour.

- Once the dough has rested, divide it into 12 even pieces and, using your hands, roll each piece into a ball.
- Roll the balls in the cinnamon sugar, making sure each piece is well covered.
- Place on the lined baking trays, leaving a gap of at least 3cm between each ball to allow them to spread during baking. Gently press down on them with the back of a spoon to flatten them slightly.
- Bake for 16–18 minutes, or until the edges of the cookies are just starting to become firm but the centres are still soft. Allow to cool on the baking trays.
- These will keep in an airtight container for 2–3 days.

SNICKERS CUPCAKES

Another addition to our range of chocolate bar cupcakes – which includes Malteser, Crunchie, Toblerone, Creme Egg – the combination of caramel, peanuts and chocolate in a Snickers bar was always going to be irresistible in cupcake form.

Makes 12 regular-sized cupcakes

CHOCOLATE SPONGE

115g dark chocolate (70% cocoa solids), broken into small pieces
85g unsalted butter, at room temperature
175g soft brown sugar
2 large eggs, separated
185g plain flour
¾ teaspoon baking powder
¾ teaspoon bicarbonate of soda
a pinch of salt
250ml semi-skimmed milk, at room temperature
1 teaspoon vanilla extract

- Preheat the oven to 180°C/160°C (fan)/350°F/gas mark 4. Line a 12-hole muffin tin with 12 muffin cases.
- Melt the chocolate in a microwaveable or heatproof bowl, either in the microwave in short bursts or over a pan of lightly simmering water on the hob. Once melted, set aside and allow to cool slightly.
- In a separate bowl and using an electric hand mixer, cream the butter and sugar together until pale and smooth.
- In a clean bowl and with clean beaters, beat the egg yolks for several minutes. Slowly add the egg yolks to the creamed butter and sugar and beat well. Then add the melted chocolate and beat well.
- Add the flour, baking powder, bicarbonate of soda and salt to another bowl and stir to combine. Pour the milk into a jug and stir in the vanilla extract.

- Add a third of the flour mixture to the egg, chocolate, butter and sugar mixture, then a third of the milk and vanilla extract. Repeat until all the flour and milk is used up, beating well after each addition.
- In a clean bowl and with clean beaters, whisk the egg whites until soft peaks start to form. Carefully fold the eggs whites into the batter, using a metal spoon. Do not beat or you will take all the air out of the cake.
- Spoon the batter evenly into the muffin cases, filling each case to about two-thirds full.
- Bake for 20–25 minutes, until the cakes are firm to the touch and an inserted skewer comes out clean.
- Leave the cupcakes to cool in their tin for about 10 minutes before turning out onto a wire rack to cool completely.

→

CARAMEL PEANUT FILLING

4 tablespoons crunchy peanut butter
4 tablespoons Salted Caramel Sauce (see recipe on page 244)

- Mix the butter and caramel sauce together in a small bowl until well combined, then set aside to cool.

CHOCOLATE PEANUT BUTTER BUTTERCREAM ICING

75g milk chocolate, broken into small pieces
90g unsalted butter, softened
30g golden syrup
30g smooth peanut butter
375g icing sugar
40ml semi-skimmed milk

- Melt the chocolate in a microwaveable or heatproof bowl, either in the microwave in short bursts or over a pan of lightly simmering water on the hob. Set aside and allow to cool.
- Put the softened butter, golden syrup and peanut butter into a separate bowl and, using an electric hand mixer, beat on a low to medium speed until smooth and thoroughly mixed. Add the icing sugar and milk, and mix together until the mixture is smooth and no lumps remain. Pour in the melted chocolate and mix on a low speed until well combined.

ASSEMBLE

3 Snickers bars, each cut into 4 pieces, to decorate

- Using a cupcake corer or small paring knife, cut out a small round (about 2–2.5cm) from the centre of each cupcake.
- Using a piping bag or spoon, fill each hole in the cupcakes with the caramel peanut filling, then ice with the chocolate peanut butter icing.
- Decorate each cupcake with a piece of Snickers.

STICKY TOFFEE COOKIES

Sticky toffee cake and biscuits are so delicious that I think it's easy to overlook how important the dates are in creating this flavour, but they really do make a difference. These biscuits are at their best when eaten fresh from the oven, when they are at their stickiest and gooiest.

Makes 18 cookies

DATE AND GINGER MIX

115g pitted dried dates, roughly chopped
150ml water
1 tablespoon fresh lemon juice
½ teaspoon bicarbonate of soda
2 pieces stem ginger, finely chopped

- Place the chopped dates and water in a pan over a medium heat. Bring to the boil and cook until no water remains (about 5 minutes) and a thick paste forms. Keep an eye on the dates to make sure they don't burn when the water has cooked off.
- Remove from the heat, then add the lemon juice, bicarbonate of soda and stem ginger and stir together until well combined. Set aside to cool while you prepare the cookie base.

COOKIE BASE

275g plain flour
½ teaspoon bicarbonate of soda
½ teaspoon salt
½ teaspoon ground ginger
120g unsalted butter, at room temperature
215g soft light brown sugar
1 large egg
½ teaspoon vanilla extract
230g Date and Ginger Mix (see above)
150g Salted Caramel Sauce (see recipe on page 244)

- Put the flour, bicarbonate of soda, salt and ground ginger into a bowl. Stir to combine, then set aside.
- In a separate bowl and using an electric hand mixer, cream the butter and sugar together until light and fluffy. Add the egg and vanilla extract and mix until well combined. Add the flour mixture and mix until it all just comes together.
- Pour in the cooled date and ginger mix and beat until thoroughly combined and the mixture comes together as a dough.
- Wrap the dough in cling film and allow to rest in the fridge for at least 1 hour, but preferably overnight, before baking.
- Preheat the oven to 180°C/160°C (fan)/350°F/ gas mark 4. Lightly grease two baking trays and line with parchment paper.
- Once the dough has rested, divide it into 18 even-sized pieces. The dough will be quite soft and wet, so dust your hands with a little flour before rolling into balls and placing on the lined baking trays. Leave a gap of about 5cm between each ball as they will spread during baking. Using your thumb, make an indent in the centre of each ball. Then place 1 teaspoon of salted caramel sauce into each indent.
- Bake for 18–20 minutes, or until the cookies are a dark golden brown on top and firm around the edges.
- Allow the cookies to stand on their trays for 5 minutes before removing to wire racks to cool.
- Any uneaten cookies can be stored in an airtight container for 2–3 days.

GLUTEN-FREE SWEET POTATO CAKE
WITH BROWN SUGAR ICING

This moist, gluten-free cake is highly recommended for its unusual but amazing flavour and pretty autumnal colours.

Makes one 20cm single-layer cake, serving 10–12

SWEET POTATO SPONGE

330g sweet potatoes
olive oil spray, for coating the potatoes
110g rice flour
2 teaspoons gluten-free baking powder
a pinch of salt
110g unsalted butter, at room temperature
155g soft light brown sugar
2 large eggs
1 teaspoon vanilla extract
100ml sour cream
40ml milk

- Preheat the oven to 180°C/160°C (fan)/350°F/ gas mark 4. Lightly grease a baking tray and line with parchment paper.
- Peel the sweet potatoes and cut into 2cm cubes. Place on the lined baking tray and spray with olive oil. Place in the oven for 25–30 minutes, or until the potatoes are soft and tender. Remove from the oven (leave the oven on) and allow to stand for 10 minutes. Then transfer to a bowl and mash with a fork. Set aside to cool before using.
- Grease a 20cm sandwich tin and line with parchment paper.
- Sift the rice flour, baking powder and salt together into a bowl, and set aside.
- In a separate bowl and using an electric hand mixer, cream the butter and sugar together until light and fluffy. Add the eggs one at a time, making sure the first one is well incorporated before adding the second. Add the vanilla with the second egg. Add the mashed sweet potato and beat until well combined. Add the sifted flour mixture and mix until well incorporated.

Finally, pour in the sour cream and milk and mix until the mixture has a smooth consistency.
- Pour the batter into the prepared cake tin and spread it out evenly.
- Bake for 40–45 minutes, or until an inserted skewer comes out clean.
- Allow the cake to stand in its tin for 15 minutes, then gently turn out onto a wire rack to cool – be careful as it is a very soft cake.

BROWN SUGAR ICING

40g unsalted butter, softened
20g brown sugar
¼ teaspoon ground cinnamon
115g cream cheese, softened
100g icing sugar

- Put the butter, brown sugar and cinnamon into a small microwaveable bowl and heat it in the microwave until the butter has melted and the sugar has dissolved. Leave to stand until the mixture is cool to the touch.
- Put the cream cheese into a bowl, then add the butter mixture and the icing sugar. Beat on a low speed until all the ingredients are combined. Scrape down the sides of the bowl and beat for a further 30 seconds until you have a smooth icing. If you are not using it straight away, place in the fridge until needed.
- When ready to serve, ice the top of the cake with the brown sugar icing.

ROCKY ROAD CHEESECAKE

Cheesecake topped with rocky road dessert – what a winning combination!

Makes one 23cm cheesecake, serving 12–15

CHEESECAKE

175g digestive biscuits
75g unsalted butter, melted
225g golden caster sugar
200g dark chocolate (70% cocoa solids), broken into small pieces
3 tablespoons cocoa powder
3 tablespoons hot water
300ml double cream
100ml sour cream
400g cream cheese, softened

- Lightly grease a deep 23cm springform cake tin and line with parchment paper.
- Blitz the digestives in a food processor bowl until they resemble fine breadcrumbs. Alternatively, place the biscuits in a large clip-seal bag, remove the excess air and bash them with the end of a rolling pin.
- Transfer the biscuit crumbs to a mixing bowl, then pour the melted butter over them and add 1 tablespoon of the caster sugar. Mix well, making sure that all the butter is mixed through the crumbs.
- Spoon this mixture evenly into the base of the springform tin, and press it down with the back of the spoon. Place in the fridge for 1 hour to set.
- Melt the chocolate in a microwaveable or heatproof bowl, either in the microwave in short bursts or over a pan of lightly simmering water on the hob. Once it has melted, set aside and allow to cool.
- In a separate small bowl, mix the cocoa powder and hot water until well combined, then set aside to cool.

- In a large bowl, beat together the double cream and sour cream with an electric hand mixer until it thickens and becomes stiff. Pour in the melted chocolate and the cocoa, then fold them in with a spatula until they are both well incorporated.
- In another bowl, cream together the cream cheese and the remaining caster sugar until smooth, then gently fold into the chocolate mixture.
- Pour this mixture over the chilled base and place in the fridge for at least 4 hours, or preferably overnight, until it is firm and set.

→

ROCKY ROAD TOPPING

30g milk chocolate
30g dark chocolate (70% cocoa solids), broken into
small pieces
4 milk chocolate digestive biscuits
40g dried sour cherries
50g roasted nuts of choice (such as almonds,
hazelnuts, peanuts or cashews)
50g mini marshmallows

- Put the milk and dark chocolates into a
  microwaveable or heatproof bowl and melt
  gently, either in the microwave in short bursts
  or over a pan of lightly simmering water on the
  hob. Set aside to cool.
- Break the chocolate digestives into bite-sized
  pieces into a bowl. Add the sour cherries, nuts
  and marshmallows. Scatter this mixture all
  over the top of the chilled cheesecake, then
  drizzle the melted chocolate over the top.
- Place the cheesecake back in the fridge
  for 15–20 minutes, or until the chocolate is set.
- Store any uneaten cheesecake in the fridge
  for 4–5 days.

Winter, with its cold, dark and often wet nights, provides us with the perfect excuse for making and eating more cakes and cookies than usual (or at least that's what I like to believe!). It's also a good time to plan ahead and prepare lots of baked goodies that can be stored in the freezer for Christmas or pre-Christmas parties or to use as edible gifts for friends and family. In this chapter you will find some of our richer and more chocolate-based recipes and a couple of dessert options in the form of our treacle tart and s'mores cheesecake. You'll also find the recipe for our salted caramel sauce, which we use in quite a few of our recipes and is a good thing to make in advance and have ready for when you need it. Winter is also a fantastic chance to spend more time with family and friends, and even bake together, especially with the children. I would recommend the Cookie Dough Cupcakes on page 208 and the Popcorn Cake on page 234 as good ones to try with children – they are quite messy to prepare but lots of fun.

Winter

GLUTEN-FREE
AVOCADO CHOCOLATE COOKIES

These vegan cookies are both gluten- and dairy-free and, although this might
seem a strange mix of flavours, the avocado and chocolate
work well together. These cookies have a similar texture to brownies.

Makes 24 cookies

COOKIES

1 soft ripe avocado (165g)
60ml olive oil
3 tablespoons apple sauce (from a jar, or purée
some apples)
130g brown sugar
85g granulated sugar
50ml soya milk
1 teaspoon vanilla extract
250g rice flour
70g cocoa powder
1 teaspoon bicarbonate of soda
½ teaspoon salt
100g dark chocolate chips (70% cocoa solids)

- In a bowl, mash the avocado with a fork until
  no large pieces remain.
- Pour in the olive oil, apple sauce and sugars,
  and mix together until it forms a smooth paste.
  Pour in the milk and vanilla extract and mix
  until well combined.
- Add the remaining ingredients and mix
  together until well incorporated and a soft
  dough forms.
- Cover the bowl with cling film and refrigerate
  for 15 minutes to allow the dough to rest.
- Preheat the oven to 180°C/160°C (fan)/350°F/
  gas mark 4. Lightly grease two baking trays
  and line with parchment paper.
- Divide the dough into 24 even-sized pieces
  and roll into balls. Flatten each ball to make
  a disc about 5mm thick. Place on the lined
  baking trays, leaving a gap of 2–3cm between
  each one.
- Bake for 10–12 minutes, until the edges of the
  cookies are firm to the touch.
- Allow to stand on the tray for 5 minutes before
  removing to wire racks to cool completely.
- Store any uneaten cookies in an airtight
  container for up to a week.

GLUTEN-FREE
BLACK FOREST CAKE

This gluten-free version of the classic Black Forest cake was created
by our head chef Daniel. It has a light, moist texture,
which complements the chocolate and cherry flavours nicely.

Makes one 20cm triple-layer cake, serving 10–12

CHOCOLATE SPONGE

9 large eggs, separated
275g soft light brown sugar
120g cocoa powder
cherry juice or cherry liqueur, for soaking the sponge

- Preheat the oven to 180°C/160°C (fan)/350°F/gas mark 4. Grease three 20cm sandwich tins and line with parchment paper.
- Using an electric hand mixer, beat the egg yolks and sugar together in a bowl until light and fluffy. Gradually add the cocoa powder and mix until it is all incorporated.
- In a separate bowl and using clean beaters, whisk the egg whites until they form stiff peaks.
- Gently fold a quarter of the whisked egg whites into the batter, to loosen it. Add the remaining egg whites and gently fold through until just combined. Be careful not to overmix as it will knock out the air from the egg whites.
- Divide the batter between the three sandwich tins and bake for 15–20 minutes, or until an inserted skewer comes out clean.
- Remove from the oven and leave the cakes to cool in their tins. They will shrink slightly and come away from the edges of the tins.
- If any of the cakes are domed, trim the tops to ensure a flat surface for stacking. Make several holes in the cooled sponge with a skewer, then brush some of the cherry juice or liqueur over the top of the cakes. Repeat two or three times, until all the juice or liqueur is used up.

BLACK CHERRY COMPOTE

1 × 410g tin pitted black cherries (in juice)
2 teaspoons cornflour
2 tablespoons cold water

- Place the cherries and their juice in a pan and bring to the boil.
- In a small bowl, mix the cornflour with the cold water, then pour into the pan of boiling cherries, stirring continuously to combine. Turn the heat down to medium and continue stirring until the mixture thickens and reaches a thick compote consistency. Pour into a heatproof bowl and leave to cool.

→

ITALIAN BUTTERCREAM

300g granulated sugar
5 tablespoons water
3 egg whites
1 teaspoon vanilla extract
400g unsalted butter, cut into cubes and softened

- Pour the sugar and water into a pan over a medium heat and bring to the boil without stirring. Allow to boil for about 3–5 minutes until a thick syrup forms.
- Meanwhile, whisk the egg whites in a clean metal bowl until stiff peaks form. With the mixer on a low or medium speed, slowly pour the syrup in a thin stream into the egg whites until it is all used up. Then add the vanilla extract and continue whisking until cool.
- Once the mixture has cooled, continue whisking and add the butter a cube at a time until it is all incorporated. The buttercream should be smooth and thick with a consistency similar to whipped cream.

ASSEMBLE

dark chocolate shavings, to decorate

- Take a third of the buttercream and place in a separate bowl. Add 2 heaped tablespoons of the black cherry compote and gently fold it in.
- Place the first cake on a cake board or serving plate and spread half of the plain buttercream on top, followed by some black cherry compote. Gently place the second cake on top and spread the cherry-coloured buttercream over the top. Then place the third cake on top and spread the remaining plain buttercream over the top. Pour any remaining black cherry compote on top of the icing and sprinkle dark chocolate shavings around it.

CINNAMON LOAF

Here, we have converted our cinnamon cupcakes into a loaf cake,
which makes a lovely edible gift for Christmas or contribution to a tea or dinner party.
There is slightly less icing on the loaf than on a cupcake,
so it's a good choice for those who prefer a less sweet cake.

Makes one 900g loaf, serving 8–10

LOAF

165g self-raising flour
1½ teaspoons ground cinnamon
a pinch of salt
150g unsalted butter, at room temperature
180g golden caster sugar
2 large eggs
½ teaspoon vanilla extract
120ml sour cream

- Preheat the oven to 180°C/160°C (fan)/350°F/ gas mark 4. Lightly grease a 900g loaf tin and line with parchment paper or with a loaf tin liner.
- Stir the flour, cinnamon and salt together in a bowl. Set aside.
- In a separate bowl and using an electric hand mixer, cream the butter and sugar for 3–5 minutes until light and fluffy. Beat in the eggs one at a time, making sure the first egg is well incorporated before adding the second. Add the vanilla extract with the second egg.
- Add half the flour mixture and mix on a low speed until combined, then add half the sour cream and beat until just mixed through. Repeat until all the flour and sour cream is used up.
- Pour the batter into the lined loaf tin and spread it out evenly.
- Bake for 40–45 minutes, or until an inserted skewer comes out clean.
- Allow to stand in the tin for 15 minutes before turning out onto a wire rack to cool.

CINNAMON CREAM CHEESE ICING

50g unsalted butter, softened
110g cream cheese, softened
225g icing sugar
1 teaspoon ground cinnamon

- Place all the ingredients in a large bowl and mix on a low speed until combined. Scrape down the sides of the bowl, then beat on a medium-high speed for 30–60 seconds until smooth.

Note Do not overmix the icing or it will become sloppy and soft. Keep refrigerated when not in use.

CINNAMON SUGAR

1 tablespoon golden caster sugar
½ teaspoon ground cinnamon

- Tip the sugar and ground cinnamon into a bowl and stir to combine.

ASSEMBLE

- Spread the cinnamon cream cheese icing all over the loaf, then sprinkle the cinnamon sugar over the top.

COOKIE DOUGH CUPCAKES

My eldest daughter, Daisy, loves cookie dough more than almost anything,
so she persuaded us to make a cupcake version.
We now sell these every Saturday at our Primrose Hill shop.

Makes 12 regular-sized cupcakes

COOKIE DOUGH

<u>Note</u> The cookie dough must be completely
frozen before using, so I would recommend
making this the day before you plan to eat it.

50g unsalted butter, at room temperature
75g light brown sugar
75g plain flour
30g dark chocolate chips (70% cocoa solids)
½ teaspoon salt
½ teaspoon vanilla extract

- Place all the ingredients in a bowl and, using
  an electric hand mixer, mix until a dough forms.
- Weigh out the dough into 20g balls and place
  in the freezer and leave overnight.

SPONGE

170g unsalted butter, softened
170g light brown sugar
3 large eggs
170g self-raising flour
45ml milk
1 teaspoon vanilla extract

- Preheat the oven to 180°C/160°C (fan)/350°F/
  gas mark 4. Line a 12-hole muffin tin with
  12 muffin cases.
- Cream together the butter and sugar in
  a bowl until light and fluffy. Add the eggs
  one at a time, making sure each one is well
  incorporated before adding the next.
- Add the flour, milk and vanilla extract and
  beat until no lumps remain.
- Spoon the batter evenly into the muffin cases
  filling each case to about two-thirds full, and
  place a piece of frozen cookie dough on top
  of each one – do not push it into the batter as
  it will sink down by itself.
- Bake for 20–25 minutes, or until the tops of
  the cakes are a light golden brown colour and
  springy to the touch. Leave to cool in their tin
  for 10 minutes, then turn out onto a wire rack
  to finish cooling.

→

COOKIE DOUGH BUTTERCREAM ICING

150g unsalted butter, at room temperature
350g icing sugar
100g light brown sugar
¼ teaspoon salt
60g sour cream
1 teaspoon vanilla extract
35g dark chocolate (70% cocoa solids), broken into small pieces

- Place all the ingredients in a bowl and beat with an electric hand mixer until combined. The icing will be slightly grainy because of the chocolate pieces.
- Spread the icing over each cupcake.

SQUASHED FLY (GARIBALDI) CUPCAKES

The classic Garibaldi biscuit, where currants are squashed between two pieces
of biscuit dough, was first sold more than 150 years ago. The flattened currants
resemble squashed flies, hence their nickname. For these cupcakes, our bakery manager,
Sally, used Marsala wine to bring an extra richness to the fruit and icing.

Makes 9 regular-sized cupcakes

MARSALA CURRANTS

100g dried currants
approx. 100ml Marsala wine, to cover the currants

- Put the currants into a bowl and pour in
  enough Marsala wine to completely cover
  the currants. Leave to soak for at least 1 hour,
  or preferably 3–4 hours. Drain the currants
  before using, reserving the wine to use in the
  cupcakes and Marsala icing.

SPONGE

120g self-raising flour
15g cornflour
½ teaspoon baking powder
115g unsalted butter, at room temperature
115g golden caster sugar
2 large eggs
1 tablespoon milk
**1 tablespoon Marsala wine (from the soaked
currants, left)**
1 batch Marsala currants, drained (see left)

- Preheat the oven to 180°C/160°C (fan)/350°F/
  gas mark 4. Line a 12-hole muffin tin with 9
  muffin cases.
- Stir the flour, cornflour and baking powder in
  a bowl, and set aside.
- In a separate bowl and using an electric hand
  mixer, cream the butter and sugar together until
  light and fluffy. Add the eggs one at a time,
  making sure the first one is well incorporated
  before adding the second. Pour in the milk and
  the Marsala wine with the second egg.
- Add the flour mixture and mix until well
  combined, then gently fold in the currants until
  well mixed through.
- Spoon the batter evenly into the muffin cases,
  filling each case to about two-thirds full.
- Bake for 20–25 minutes until the tops of the
  cakes are golden brown and an inserted skewer
  comes out clean.
- Allow to stand in their tins for 10 minutes before
  turning out onto wire racks to cool.

MARSALA BUTTERCREAM ICING

85g unsalted butter, at room temperature
30ml milk
20ml Marsala wine (from the soaked currants, page 212)
375g icing sugar

- In a bowl, beat together the butter, milk and Marsala wine until smooth. Add half the icing sugar and beat on a low speed until combined. Scrape down the sides of the bowl, then add the remaining icing sugar and beat on a low speed until well incorporated. Turn up to a medium speed and beat for a further 30 seconds until smooth.

DECORATE

15 Garibaldi biscuits, cut in half

- Ice the cupcakes with the Marsala icing, then place half a Garibaldi biscuit on top of each one.

GLUTEN-FREE
SALTED CARAMEL BROWNIE

A gluten-free brownie which combines two of our favourite ingredients –
salted caramel and chocolate.

Makes one 33×23cm tray, serving 15

BROWNIE

Note To make the gluten-free self-raising flour
for this recipe, mix 140g gluten-free plain flour,
1½ teaspoons gluten-free baking powder and
¼ teaspoon salt together in a bowl.

300g unsalted butter
250g golden caster sugar
40g cocoa powder
150g gluten-free self-raising flour (see above)
¼ teaspoon gluten-free baking powder
120g dark chocolate chips (70% cocoa solids)
250g caramel chocolate chips
3 large eggs, lightly beaten
1 batch Salted Caramel Sauce (see recipe on page 244)
fleur de sel, for sprinkling

- Preheat the oven to 180°C/160°C (fan)/350°F/
  gas mark 4. Lightly grease the base and sides
  of a 33 × 23cm baking tray and line with
  parchment paper.
- Melt the butter in the microwave or in a small
  pan on the hob. Set aside to cool slightly.
- Put the sugar, cocoa powder, flour, baking
  powder and chocolate chips into a large bowl.
  Stir with a wooden spoon to combine all the
  ingredients, then make a well in the centre.
- Pour the melted butter into the well in the dry
  ingredients and stir until well combined. Add
  the eggs and stir to combine.
- Pour the mixture into the prepared baking
  tray and spread it out evenly. Spoon the salted
  caramel sauce over the top, then use a skewer
  to swirl it in – do not mix it in completely, you
  just want to create a marble effect on the
  surface. Sprinkle a little fleur de sel over the top.
- Bake on the middle rack of the oven for
  30–35 minutes until the brownie is set in the
  middle. An inserted skewer should not come
  out clean but be slightly fudgey. Do not overbake.
- Allow to cool before cutting into squares.

KIT KAT BROWNIE

My daughter Daisy developed this rich, chocolatey brownie where the wafers and Kit Kats add a wonderfully crunchy texture. Hard to stop after just one piece!

Makes one 33×23cm tray, serving 15

BROWNIE

375g wafer biscuits with chocolate filling
300g unsalted butter, melted
250g golden caster sugar
40g cocoa powder
150g plain flour
¼ teaspoon baking powder
3 large eggs, lightly beaten
9 x four-finger Kit Kat chocolate bars

- Preheat the oven to 180°C/160°C (fan)/350°F/ gas mark 4.
- Lightly grease the base and sides of a 33 × 23cm baking tray and line with parchment paper. Place a layer of wafer biscuits on the base of the tray, and set aside.
- Melt the butter in a microwaveable bowl in the microwave or in a pan on the hob, and set aside to cool slightly.
- Put the sugar, cocoa powder, flour and baking powder into a bowl. Stir with a wooden spoon to combine all the ingredients, then make a well in the centre.
- Pour the slightly cooled melted butter and the eggs into the well in the dry ingredients and stir until well combined.
- Carefully pour half of this batter on top of the wafers in the bottom of the tray and spread it out. Then lay the Kit Kat bars lengthways over the batter. Pour the remaining batter over the Kit Kats and spread it out, making sure the Kit Kats are well covered.
- Bake for 30–35 minutes until the brownie is firm to the touch and an inserted skewer comes out clean.
- Allow to cool in its tray before removing and cutting into squares.

MARS BAR CUPCAKES

When developing these cupcakes, we wanted to be sure they had an authentic Mars Bar taste, which meant the caramel and nougat were a little fiddly to perfect. So these will take a little longer to prepare than some of our other recipes, but I think you will agree they are worth the extra time.

Makes 16 regular-sized cupcakes

CHOCOLATE SPONGE

115g dark chocolate (70% cocoa solids), broken into small pieces
85g unsalted butter, at room temperature
175g soft brown sugar
185g plain flour
¾ teaspoon baking powder
¾ teaspoon bicarbonate of soda
a pinch of salt
250ml semi-skimmed milk, at room temperature
1 teaspoon vanilla extract
2 large eggs, separated

Note You will need a sugar thermometer to make the caramel.

- Preheat the oven to 180°C/160°C (fan)/350°F/gas mark 4. Line two 12-hole muffin tins with 16 muffin cases.
- Melt the chocolate in a microwaveable or heatproof bowl, either in the microwave in short bursts or over a pan of lightly simmering water on the hob. Be careful not to let the chocolate burn. Leave to cool slightly.
- In a bowl and using an electric hand mixer, cream the butter and sugar together until pale and smooth.
- In a separate bowl, combine the flour, baking powder, bicarbonate of soda and salt. Pour the milk into a jug and stir in the vanilla extract. Set aside.
- In another bowl and with clean beaters, beat the egg yolks for several minutes. Slowly add to the creamed butter and sugar and beat well.

Next, add the melted chocolate and beat well. Add a third of the flour mixture and then a third of the milk and vanilla, beating well after each addition. Repeat until all the flour and milk mixtures have been incorporated.
- In a clean bowl, whisk the egg whites until soft peaks start to form. Carefully fold the eggs whites into the batter, using a metal spoon. Do not beat or you will take all the air out of the cake.
- Spoon the batter evenly into the muffin cases, filling each case to about two-thirds full.
- Bake for 20–25 minutes, until an inserted skewer comes out clean. Leave the cakes to cool in their tins for 10 minutes before removing to wire racks to continue cooling.

SOFT CARAMEL

200g granulated sugar
40g golden syrup
40ml water
140ml double cream
30g unsalted butter, at room temperature
½ teaspoon salt
½ teaspoon vanilla extract

Note Be very careful when making the caramel, as it is very hot and will burn if it comes into contact with the skin.

- Put the sugar, golden syrup and water into a heavy-bottomed pan and place over a low heat until the sugar dissolves. Turn the heat up to medium and bring to the boil. Brush down the sides of the pan with a pastry brush dipped in cold water to dissolve any sugar crystals that may have formed on the sides. As soon as the mixture starts to boil, attach the sugar thermometer to the pan. Do not stir the syrup after it starts to boil.
- While the sugar syrup is boiling, pour the cream, butter and salt into a microwaveable bowl and heat in the microwave briefly until the mixture is warm and the butter has melted. Set aside until ready to use.
- Once the sugar syrup reaches 121°C, remove from the heat and pour in the cream in a very slow and steady stream, stirring continuously with a wooden spoon. Take care when pouring in the cream, as the mixture will start to bubble vigorously and let off a lot of steam.
- Once all the cream has been added, place the pan back on the hob over a low to medium heat and bring it back to the boil without stirring. Boil until the caramel reaches 121°C and is an amber golden colour.
- Immediately pour the syrup into a heatproof bowl, then stir in the vanilla extract and set aside while you prepare the nougat icing.

NOUGAT ICING

Note This icing needs to be used straight away, so only start to make it when the cupcakes are ready to be iced.

2 egg whites
2 tablespoons honey
260g granulated sugar
2 tablespoons water
2 teaspoons vanilla extract

- Put the egg whites, honey, sugar and water into a heatproof bowl and, using an electric hand mixer, beat for 30 seconds on a high speed until the mixture is opaque, white and foamy.
- Place the bowl over a pan of barely simmering water – the water should have steam coming from the top with only a few bubbles appearing.
- Immediately after placing the bowl over the pan, continue beating with the mixer on a high speed for a further 10–12 minutes, making sure the water is barely at a simmer. If it does start simmering or boiling, turn down the heat and add a little cold water to the pan. If the bowl gets too hot, the mixture will start to cook and form a layer on the bottom of the bowl, which will result in small particles throughout the nougat icing.
- After 10–12 minutes, the mixture should form stiff peaks that stand straight up when the beaters are stopped and removed.
- Remove the bowl from the pan, add the vanilla extract and continue beating on high speed for a further minute. During this time, the mixture will thicken further and become shinier.

ASSEMBLE

4 Mars Bars, each cut into 4 pieces, to decorate

- When the soft caramel is cool enough to handle, but still warm and soft, place a tablespoonful on top of each cupcake. Using your fingertips or the back of a spoon dipped in cold water, lightly press and spread the caramel on top of the cupcake, covering it completely. Then ice each cupcake with the nougat icing and top with a piece of Mars Bar.

CHOCOLATE MINT SLICE

This recipe and the one for the Mint Chocolate Chip Loaf on page 262 were both developed by our former business manager, Faye, back in her home country of New Zealand. She remains an important part of Primrose Bakery, even from so far away, and the first time we made this chocolate mint slice in the bakery kitchen, we wished she had been here with us, as it was so delicious, especially served straight from the fridge which made it extra crunchy.

Makes one 33×23cm tray, serving 15

BISCUIT BASE

1 × 300g packet Rich Tea biscuits
4 tablespoons cocoa powder
100g soft light brown sugar
1 tablespoon golden syrup
1 teaspoon vanilla extract
150g unsalted butter, melted

- Lightly grease a 33 × 23cm baking tray and line with parchment paper.
- Put the biscuits in the bowl of a food processor and pulse until they are coarsely ground and in small chunks. Do not over-process the biscuits as you don't want them too fine.
- Put the cocoa powder, brown sugar, golden syrup and vanilla extract into a bowl. Pour in the melted butter and mix together until well combined. Add the crushed biscuits and mix again until well combined.
- Pour this mixture into the prepared baking tray, then press it down evenly over the base with the back of a spoon or your hands.
- Cover with cling film and place in the fridge for 30–60 minutes to allow it to set.

MINT FILLING

150g unsalted butter
280g icing sugar
2 tablespoons double cream
1 teaspoon peppermint extract
4–5 drops green gel food colouring

- Soften the butter in the microwave for 5–10 seconds at a time, until it forms a smooth paste. Be careful not to melt the butter.
- Put the icing sugar into a bowl, then add the softened butter, double cream and peppermint extract and, using an electric hand mixer, mix together until it has a nice thick consistency. Add more peppermint extract if you want a mintier flavour.
- Add the green food colouring and mix until well combined.
- Remove the biscuit base from the fridge and spread the mint filling evenly on top. Re-cover with cling film, then place in the fridge for 1 hour to set.

CHOCOLATE TOPPING

200g chocolate mint cream biscuits
250g dark chocolate (70% cocoa solids), broken into small pieces

- Put the biscuits into the bowl of a food processor and pulse until they resemble coarse breadcrumbs.
- Melt the chocolate in a microwaveable or heatproof bowl, either in the microwave in short bursts or over a pan of lightly simmering water on the hob. Be careful not to let the chocolate burn. Leave to cool for 5 minutes.
- Remove the biscuit base from the fridge. Pour the melted chocolate over the mint filling, and spread it out evenly.
- Sprinkle the biscuit crumbs over the melted chocolate.
- Re-cover with cling film and place back in the fridge for a further 30–60 minutes, or until the chocolate has set.
- Cut into slices and if not eating straight away, store in an airtight container at room temperature or in the fridge.

PARSNIP, PEAR AND SESAME BUNDT CAKE

This is a lovely fresh and fruity cake and it looks so pretty when made in the Bundt tin, with its fluted circular shape.

Makes one 20cm Bundt cake, serving 10–12

PARSNIP PEAR MIX

3 ripe pears (approx. 320g)
240g parsnips, peeled
1 tablespoon sesame seeds
20g unsalted butter
50g soft light brown sugar

- Peel and core the pears, then cut into 1cm cubes. Place in a bowl and set aside.
- Using the large side of a grater, grate the parsnips into a separate bowl and add the sesame seeds.
- Heat the butter and sugar in a medium pan over a medium heat until the butter has melted and the sugar has dissolved. Add the grated parsnip and sesame mixture, stirring constantly. Turn the heat up to high and cook until the mixture starts to become transparent (about 2–3 minutes).
- Remove from the heat, add the pears and stir through. Set aside to cool while you prepare the sponge.

SPONGE

255g self-raising flour
½ teaspoon baking powder
¼ teaspoon salt
160g unsalted butter, at room temperature
185g golden caster sugar
2 large eggs
1 teaspoon vanilla extract
1 batch Parsnip Pear Mix (see above)

- Preheat the oven to 180°C/160°C (fan)/350°F/gas mark 4. Generously grease a 20cm Bundt cake tin, making sure all the grooves are well greased.
- Stir the flour, baking powder and salt together in a bowl and set aside.
- In a separate bowl and using an electric hand mixer, cream the butter and sugar together until light and fluffy. Add the eggs one at a time, making sure the first one is well incorporated before adding the second. Add the vanilla extract with the second egg.
- Add the flour mixture and mix until it just comes together, then fold in the parsnip pear mix, and mix until well combined.
- Pour the batter into the prepared Bundt tin.
- Bake for 40–45 minutes or until the cake is golden brown on top and an inserted skewer comes out clean.
- Allow to cool in its tin for 10 minutes, then turn out onto a wire rack to cool completely.

PEAR GLAZE

1 ripe pear
2 tablespoons golden caster sugar
80ml pear nectar (from a tin or jar)
1 teaspoon fresh lemon juice

- Peel and core the pear, then cut into 8 pieces. Place in a small pan and add the remaining ingredients. Cook on a low to medium heat until the pear is soft and tender.
- Using a fork, mash the pear pieces, then allow the mixture to simmer for a further 2–3 minutes until it becomes a thick syrup. Leave to cool for 10 minutes before drizzling over the cake.

PEANUT BUTTER BROWNIE CUPS

Our super-talented Mongolian chef, Manda, developed these for us.
She has worked at the bakery almost as long as me and, without her, things would
not run nearly as smoothly.

Makes 12 brownie cups

BROWNIE CUPS

24 Oreo cookies
3 tablespoons smooth peanut butter
150g unsalted butter
150g dark chocolate (70% cocoa solids), broken into
small pieces
230g golden caster sugar
115g plain flour
30g cocoa powder
¼ teaspoon baking powder
a pinch of salt
3 large eggs
icing sugar, for dusting (optional)

- Preheat the oven to 180°C/160°C (fan)/350°F/
  gas mark 4. Line a 12-hole muffin tin with
  12 muffin cases.
- Take one Oreo cookie and spread one side
  with peanut butter. Top with another cookie,
  to make a sandwich, and place in one of
  the muffin cases. Continue like this until all
  12 cases are filled with cookie sandwiches.
  Set aside.
- In a microwaveable or heatproof bowl, gently
  melt the 150g of butter and dark chocolate
  together, either in the microwave or over
  a pan of lightly simmering water on the hob.
  Set aside to cool slightly.
- Combine the sugar, plain flour, cocoa powder,
  baking powder and salt in a separate bowl. Stir
  well and make a well in the centre.
- Pour the melted butter and chocolate into the
  well in the dry ingredients and mix until smooth.
  Add the eggs and mix until well combined.
- Spoon the batter evenly over the cookie
  sandwiches and spread it out inside the cases
  so that the batter surrounds each sandwich.
- Bake for 12–15 minutes until the cookies are
  firm to the touch and an inserted skewer
  comes out clean. Do not overbake.
- Leave to cool, then dust with icing sugar
  before serving if desired.

PEANUT BUTTER AND OREO BROWNIE

Subtly different from the brownie cups in the previous recipe, this rich brownie looks divine piled high in pieces on a plate where the stripes of peanut butter, Oreo and brownie are clearly visible. We sell this on a regular basis in both the shops.

Makes one 33×23cm tray, serving 15

BASE

225g plain flour
¾ teaspoon bicarbonate of soda
½ teaspoon baking powder
¼ teaspoon salt
170g golden caster sugar
115g soft light brown sugar
75g milk chocolate chips
125g unsalted butter, softened
250g chunky peanut butter
1 large egg
1 tablespoon semi-skimmed milk
24 Oreo cookies

- Preheat the oven to 180°C/160°C (fan)/350°F/ gas mark 4. Lightly grease the base and sides of a 33 × 23cm baking tray and line with parchment paper.
- Stir the flour, bicarbonate of soda, baking powder and salt together in a bowl, then add the sugars and chocolate chips and make a well in the centre.
- Add the softened butter and the peanut butter to the well and mix together with an electric hand mixer until it starts to form crumbs. Add the egg and milk, then mix until a soft dough forms.
- Tip the dough into the lined tray and spread it out until the base is evenly covered.
- Arrange a single layer of Oreo cookies on top of the dough. Set aside while you prepare the brownie mixture.

BROWNIE

160g golden caster sugar
60g dark chocolate chips (70% cocoa solids)
125g milk chocolate chips
25g cocoa powder
100g plain flour
200g unsalted butter, melted
2 large eggs

- Tip the sugar and all the chocolate chips into a bowl, add the cocoa powder and plain flour. Using a wooden spoon, stir to combine all the ingredients, then make a well in the centre.
- Pour the melted butter into the well, followed by the eggs, and mix until thoroughly combined.
- Spread the brownie mixture carefully and evenly over the top of the Oreos in the baking tray.
- Bake for 35–40 minutes, until the top is firm to the touch round the edges, but still slightly soft in the centre. An inserted skewer should come out still a little sticky with batter. Do not overbake, so it maintains its fudgey brownie texture.
- Allow to cool completely before cutting into squares.

POPCORN CAKE

Popcorn has seen a huge increase in popularity over the last few years, and my favourite flavours are salted caramel or sweet and salty mix. There are lots of amazing popcorn producers out there now, but we have always enjoyed Joe & Seph's Gourmet Popcorn and we worked with them on this recipe. This family business started in 2010 and all their popcorn is handmade in London using only natural ingredients. They now make over 40 flavours, which are available nationwide in some supermarkets and specialist shops.

Makes one 23cm single-layer cake, serving 12–15

SPONGE

290g self-raising flour
¼ teaspoon salt
250g unsalted butter, at room temperature
210g golden caster sugar
3 large eggs
1 teaspoon vanilla extract
200ml whole milk

- Preheat the oven to 180°C/160°C (fan)/350°F/gas mark 4. Lightly grease a deep 23cm baking tin and line with parchment paper.
- Put the flour and salt into a bowl, stir to combine, then set aside.
- In a separate bowl and using an electric hand mixer, cream the butter and sugar together for 3–5 minutes until pale and fluffy. Add the eggs one at a time, mixing well between each addition. Add the vanilla extract with the last egg.
- Add half the flour mixture and beat until well incorporated, then pour in half the milk and mix until smooth. Repeat until all of the flour and milk is incorporated.
- Pour the batter into the prepared tin and spread it out evenly.
- Bake on the middle rack of the oven for 45–50 minutes, until the cake is golden brown on top and an inserted skewer comes out clean.
- Allow to cool in its tin for 15 minutes before turning onto a wire rack to cool completely.

DARK CHOCOLATE GANACHE

300g dark chocolate (70% cocoa solids), broken into small pieces
250ml double cream

- Put the chocolate into a heatproof bowl and set aside.
- Heat the cream in a small pan over a low to medium heat until it starts to simmer. Be careful not to allow it to boil. Once the cream starts to simmer, immediately pour it over the chocolate.
- Let it stand for 30–60 seconds, then stir with a wooden spoon or rubber spatula until all the chocolate has melted and the mixture is smooth.
- Allow it to cool to room temperature.

ASSEMBLE

110g Joe & Seph's Smooth Caramel & Belgian Chocolate Popcorn
110g Joe & Seph's Salted Caramel Popcorn

- Put all the popcorn into a bowl and mix together.
- Ice the sides and the top of the cooled cake with the chocolate ganache.
- Cover the sides and the top of the cake with the popcorn, gently pushing it into the ganache to ensure it sticks.
- This cake is best served immediately, as the popcorn will start to go soft over time.

PRUNE AND ARMAGNAC CUPCAKES

Prunes and Armagnac is a classic flavour combination and is used in many desserts and some savoury dishes the world over, so of course it seemed a good idea to try it out in a cupcake. This does have a rich, alcoholic flavour, so perhaps not one for the children!

Makes 12 regular-sized cupcakes

SPONGE

80g pitted prunes, chopped
4 tablespoons Armagnac, plus 2 tablespoons
125g dark chocolate (70% cocoa solids), broken into small pieces
125g unsalted butter
150g golden caster sugar
4 large eggs
75g self-raising flour
¼ teaspoon baking powder

- Place the chopped prunes in a small bowl and pour the 4 tablespoons of Armagnac over them. Cover the bowl with cling film and leave to soak for 2–3 hours.
- Preheat the oven to 180°C/160°C (fan)/350°F/gas mark 4. Line a 12-hole muffin tin with 12 muffin cases.
- Gently melt the chocolate, either in a microwaveable bowl in the microwave or in a heatproof bowl set over a pan of lightly simmering water on the hob. Set aside to cool slightly.
- In a large bowl, cream together the butter and sugar until light and frothy, using an electric hand mixer. Add the slightly cooled melted chocolate, and beat again. Add the eggs one at a time, beating well after each addition. Add the flour and baking powder and beat well, then add the remaining 2 tablespoons of Armagnac and beat again.
- Drain the prunes lightly (do not squeeze out all the Armagnac) and reserve the liquid (you will be using this in the icing later). Gently fold the prunes into the chocolate batter.
- Spoon the batter evenly into the muffin cases and bake for 20 minutes, or until an inserted skewer comes out clean.
- Allow to cool in their tin for 10 minutes, then transfer to a wire rack to cool completely.

ARMAGNAC CREAM ICING

300ml double cream
approx. 4 tablespoons Armagnac (reserved from the prune soak)
4 tablespoons icing sugar, sifted

- Beat all the ingredients together in a bowl until medium-stiff peaks form. Be careful not to overbeat the cream or it will become clumpy and grainy.
- Ice each cupcake with the Armagnac cream icing and serve immediately.

PUFFED RICE CAKE

This very sweet and sticky colourful cake is simple to put together and requires no baking. It would be fun to make this with the children one afternoon and it's ideal for a children's birthday party. It will keep well in an airtight container.

Makes one 20cm single-layer cake, serving 10–12

CAKE

100g unsalted butter, cut into cubes
300g pink and white marshmallows
125g Kellogg's Fruit Loops
100g puffed rice cereal (such as Rice Krispies)
140g chocolate M&M's of your choice
120g Gummy Bear sweets
multi-coloured sprinkles, to decorate (optional)

- Lightly grease the base and sides of a deep 20cm springform cake tin and line with parchment paper.
- Put the butter into a microwaveable or heatproof bowl and gently melt, either in the microwave or over a pan of lightly simmering water on the hob. Once the butter has melted, add the marshmallows and continue heating until they are soft and become liquid.
- In a separate bowl, mix together the Fruit Loops, puffed rice, M&M's and Gummy Bears. Add the marshmallow mixture and mix together with a wooden spoon until well combined.
- Pour the mixture into the cake tin and gently press it into the tin, making sure the top is flat. Decorate with some colourful sprinkles if desired.
- Leave to set in the cake tin for at least 1 hour, or until set.
- Transfer to a cake board or serving plate, peel off the baking paper and cut into slices.

SALTED CARAMEL LAYER CAKE

This is one of our bestselling cakes, and the recipe below includes the method for making our Salted Caramel Sauce, which we use in many of our other recipes. I recommend you keep a jar of it in your kitchen so you have some to hand to use in your baking or to pour over a bowl of ice cream for an easy dessert.

Makes one 20cm two-layer cake, serving 10–12

SALTED CARAMEL SAUCE

110g granulated sugar
3 tablespoons water
125ml double cream
1 teaspoon fleur de sel

Note This is a very hot liquid, so please be careful when making it.

- Pour the sugar and water into a clean, medium pan over a medium heat. Do not stir the mixture as this will cause the sugar syrup to crystallise. Swirl the pan occasionally and gently until all the sugar has dissolved.
- Turn the heat up to high and let the syrup boil until it turns a lovely golden colour.
- While the sugar syrup is boiling, pour the cream into a separate pan over a medium heat and add the fleur de sel. Heat until it starts 'smoking' (about 80°C, if using a sugar thermometer). Turn the heat down to medium-low and stir occasionally to prevent a skin from forming on top of the cream. Do not let it boil.
- Once the sugar syrup is ready, remove it from the heat and immediately add a small portion of the hot cream. Stir quickly with a wooden spoon to prevent it from sticking to the bottom of the pan. Be careful when adding the cream, as it will bubble up and rise very quickly, letting off a lot of hot steam, and may splutter.
- Gradually add the remainder of the cream in small amounts. Keep stirring while the cream is being added.
- Pour the sauce into a heatproof bowl and set it aside to cool while you prepare the sponge.

→

SPONGE

225g golden caster sugar
1 teaspoon baking powder
210g self-raising flour
25g cornflour
225g unsalted butter, at room temperature
4 large eggs
1 teaspoon vanilla extract
3 tablespoons semi-skimmed milk

- Preheat the oven to 180°C/160°C (fan)/350°F/gas mark 4. Grease two 20cm sandwich tins and line with parchment paper.
- Put the sugar, baking powder, flour and cornflour into a food processor bowl and pulse until evenly combined. Add the remaining ingredients and process briefly until combined. Don't be tempted to leave the processor on and walk away from it as the batter will quickly overmix and the resulting cake will have a heavier texture.
- Divide the batter evenly between the two cake tins and bake for about 25 minutes until the cakes have risen, are golden brown on top and an inserted skewer comes out clean. Leave to cool in their tins for about 10 minutes before turning out onto a wire rack to cool completely.

SALTED CARAMEL BUTTERCREAM ICING

150g unsalted butter, softened
150g Salted Caramel Sauce (see page 244)
300g icing sugar

- Mix the butter and caramel sauce together in a bowl until smooth.
- Add the icing sugar and beat on a low speed, using an electric hand mixer, until all the icing sugar is incorporated. Then beat for a further 30–60 seconds on a medium speed until the icing is smooth and lump-free.

ASSEMBLE

16–20 pieces caramel-filled chocolate (such as Galaxy Caramel)
3–4 Werthers Originals sweets, crushed into small pieces using a rolling pin
fleur de sel

- If any of the cakes are domed, trim the tops to ensure they are as flat as possible before stacking.
- Put one cake on a cake board or serving plate. Spread some salted caramel icing over the top. Neatly arrange the pieces of caramel-filled chocolate in a circle around the edge of the cake.
- Spread a little icing on the bottom of the second cake (this will help the cake to stick to the chocolate), then place on top of the first cake. Use the remaining icing to ice the top of the cake.
- Sprinkle the crushed Werthers and a little fleur de sel over the top.
- Cut into slices and serve with any remaining salted caramel sauce.

S'MORES CHEESECAKE

This is quite a rich cheesecake, so it would be a good dessert to serve around Christmas time. A s'more is a popular American treat, consisting of toasted marshmallow and a layer of chocolate sandwiched between two biscuits. To save time, you can prepare the cheesecake base and filling the day before you plan to eat it.

Makes one 23cm cheesecake, serving 12–15

BASE

175g digestive biscuits
75g unsalted butter, melted
1 tablespoon golden caster sugar

- Lightly grease a 23cm springform cake tin and line with parchment paper.
- Blitz the digestives in a food processor until they resemble fine breadcrumbs. Alternatively, place them in a large clip-seal bag, remove the excess air and bash with the end of a rolling pin.
- Put the digestive crumbs into a bowl, pour the melted butter over them and add the caster sugar. Mix well, making sure all the butter is mixed through the crumbs. Tip the mixture into the prepared cake tin and press it down into the base with the back of a spoon. Place in the fridge for 1 hour to set.

FILLING

200g dark chocolate (70% cocoa solids), broken into small pieces
3 tablespoons cocoa powder
3 tablespoons hot water
300ml double cream
100ml sour cream
400g cream cheese, at room temperature
225g golden caster sugar

- Put the chocolate into a microwaveable or heatproof bowl and melt gently, either in the microwave in short bursts or over a pan of lightly simmering water on the hob. Once the chocolate has melted, set aside and allow to cool.
- In a separate small bowl, mix together the cocoa powder and hot water until well combined, and set aside to cool.
- In a large bowl, beat the double cream and sour cream together until it thickens and becomes stiff. Pour the cooled melted chocolate and cocoa mixtures into the cream and fold in with a spatula until well incorporated.
- In another bowl, beat the cream cheese and sugar together until smooth, then gently fold into the chocolate mixture.
- Pour this over the chilled base and place in the fridge for at least 4 hours, or preferably overnight, until firm and set.

MARSHMALLOW TOPPING

60g granulated sugar
40g golden syrup
¾ tablespoon water
1 large egg white
¼ teaspoon vanilla extract

- Heat the sugar, golden syrup and water in a small pan over a high heat until the mixture reaches soft-ball stage. This is when the bubbles in the mixture almost start to stick together and would drop off a spoon in a smooth, slow stream. This will take about 1½–2 minutes. Remove from the heat.
- Meanwhile, in a clean bowl and using an electric hand mixer, whisk the egg white until soft peaks begin to form. Still beating on a low speed, slowly pour the hot sugar syrup in a steady stream into the egg white. Continue to beat on a low speed until all the hot syrup is in the mixing bowl.
- Increase the speed to medium-high and continue beating the mixture until it becomes thick, glossy and cool. Add the vanilla extract towards the end of the mixing process.

ASSEMBLE

digestive biscuits, crushed, for sprinkling on top

- Remove the cheesecake from its tin and place on a cake board or serving plate.
- Spread the marshmallow over the top of the cheesecake.
- If you have a small cook's blowtorch, quickly flame the surface of the marshmallow so it's nice and caramelised.
- To finish, sprinkle the crushed digestive biscuits over the top.

TREACLE TART

It seems as if I have a lot of 'favourite' cakes and desserts – so it's just as well
I do the job I do! – but treacle tart is one of my all-time favourites.
I am not sure why it has taken us five books to get our own Primrose Bakery version!
A slice of this tart served with cream or ice cream is heaven.

Makes one 23cm tart, serving 12–15

SHORTCRUST PASTRY BASE

295g plain flour
70g golden caster sugar
¼ teaspoon salt
165g unsalted butter, cut into cubes
1 large egg
1–2 tablespoons chilled water

- Place the flour, sugar and salt in a food processor bowl and pulse for 20 seconds to combine. Add the cubed butter and pulse until the mixture resembles coarse breadcrumbs.
- Add the egg and 1 tablespoon of the chilled water and process until a dough starts to form. Only add the extra water if required.
- Turn the dough out onto a lightly floured surface and gently knead several times to break down any pockets of flour.
- Form the dough into a ball, then flatten into a disc. Wrap in cling film and place in the fridge to rest for 25–30 minutes.
- Preheat the oven to 180°C/160°C (fan)/350°F/ gas mark 4. Lightly grease and flour a 23cm loose-bottomed tart tin.
- Remove the pastry from the fridge and roll it out on a lightly floured surface to about 5mm thick.
- Line the tart tin with the pastry, trim the excess and then prick the pastry on the base of the tin several times with a fork. Place the tart back in the fridge for 10 minutes.

- Remove from the fridge, then place a large piece of parchment paper on top of the pastry and weight it down with baking beans or rice. Bake for 15 minutes, then remove the parchment paper and beans or rice and bake for a further 5–10 minutes until the pastry is a light golden brown.
- Remove from the oven (leave the oven on) and allow to stand while you prepare the treacle filling.

TREACLE FILLING

160g sourdough bread
175g unsalted butter
520g golden syrup
60g black treacle
½ teaspoon salt
zest of 1 lemon
juice of ½ lemon
1 large egg
50ml double cream

- Blitz the soughdough bread in a food processor bowl until it resembles breadcrumbs. Pour into a large, heatproof bowl and set aside.
- Melt the butter in a pan over a medium heat until it starts to foam, then pour in the golden syrup and black treacle and stir to combine. Add the salt, lemon zest and juice and mix well. Once the mixture is warm, remove from the heat, pour it over the breadcrumbs and stir until all the ingredients are incorporated. Then add in the egg and cream and stir until combined.
- Pour the mixture into the tart shell and spread it out evenly.
- Bake for 20 minutes, then turn the oven down to 140°C/120°C (fan)/275°F/gas mark 1. Bake for a further 15–20 minutes, until the pastry is golden brown and the filling is set but still wobbly in the middle.
- Allow to cool before serving, or you can serve while still a little warm.

TURTLE SLICE

Turtles are an American confectionery consisting of chocolate, caramel and pecans, but I was attracted to them mostly because of their name and the fact that the finished chocolates do look like turtles, with the pecans serving as their feet and head. This slice makes 12 turtle squares, and these are good served as after-dinner chocolates or would make a lovely edible gift.

Makes one 33×23cm tray, serving 12

CHOCOLATE BASE

90g plain flour
45g cocoa powder
100g unsalted butter, at room temperature
105g golden caster sugar
2 large eggs
½ teaspoon vanilla extract

- Preheat the oven to 180°C/160°C (fan)/350°F/ gas mark 4. Lightly grease a 33 × 23cm baking tray and line with parchment paper.
- Stir the flour and cocoa powder together in a bowl, and set aside.
- In a separate bowl and using an electric hand mixer, cream the butter and sugar together until light and fluffy. Add the eggs one at a time, making sure the first one is well incorporated before adding the second. Add the vanilla extract with the second egg.
- Add the flour and cocoa mixture and mix until thoroughly combined.
- Spread this mixture evenly over the base of the lined baking tray.
- Bake for 12–15 minutes, until the base is firm and the centre springs back to the touch. Allow to cool in the tray.

SOFT CARAMEL

160g granulated sugar
30g golden syrup
2 tablespoons water
115ml double cream
20g unsalted butter
¼ teaspoon salt
¼ teaspoon vanilla extract

- Follow the method for making the Soft Caramel on page 222, using the quantities listed above.

CHOCOLATE TOPPING

190g milk chocolate, broken into small pieces
100g dark chocolate (70% cocoa solids), broken into small pieces
1 teaspoon vegetable oil

- Place all the ingredients in a microwaveable or heatproof bowl and gently melt, either in the microwave in 20–30 second bursts or over a pan of lightly simmering water on the hob.

ASSEMBLE

60 pecan halves (approx. 80g), plus 6

- Spread a thin layer of chocolate topping on top of the chocolate base.
- You will be making 12 'turtles', with 4 lengthways and 3 across the width, spaced out evenly across the base.
- Each turtle is made up of 5 pecan halves. Make an 'X' shape with 4 of the pecan halves, placing them directly on top of the base, flat-side down. Now dip the flat side of the fifth pecan into the chocolate topping and place it right in the middle of the cross; this will be the shell of the turtle.
- Repeat these steps until all 12 turtles have been made, then put the tray in the fridge for 15 minutes, or until the chocolate has set.

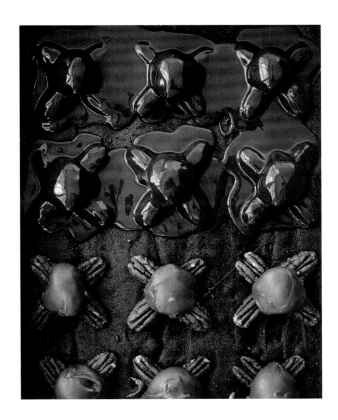

- When the soft caramel is thick and close to setting, place 1 heaped teaspoonful on top of each turtle shell. The caramel should not be runny and should just cover each shell. Place the tray in the fridge again for 15 minutes.
- Pour the remainder of the chocolate topping directly over the top of each turtle, making sure each one is completely covered. The chocolate should still be melted but not warm or it will melt the caramel. Break the 6 remaining pecan halves in half and carefully place one in each turtle to form its 'head'. Then, using a small palette knife, carefully spread any excess chocolate all over the base, between the turtles.
- Place the whole tray in the fridge for 30 minutes, or until the chocolate has set.
- Cut into squares, with a turtle in the middle of each piece.
- These are best eaten on the same day, but will keep for 2–3 days in an airtight container.

CHAI LATTE CUPCAKES

Chai is sweet, spiced Indian tea and chai latte has become a fashionable
hot drink over the last few years. It seemed a good flavour to interpret as a cupcake and the combination
of sweet and spicy works well here.

Makes 10 regular-sized cupcakes

CHAI LATTE MIX

30g skimmed milk powder
70g non-dairy creamer powder or coffee
whitener powder
150g granulated sugar
15g instant tea granules
½ teaspoon ground ginger
½ teaspoon ground cinnamon
¼ teaspoon ground cardamom

- Place all the ingredients in a food processer bowl and pulse until smooth and well combined.
- Any unused chai latte mix can be stored in an airtight container in a cool, dry place for up to 2 weeks.

CHAI LATTE SPONGE

112g plain flour
¾ teaspoon baking powder
¼ teaspoon salt
125ml semi-skimmed milk
1 teaspoon vanilla extract
115g unsalted butter, at room temperature
70g golden caster sugar
110g Chai Latte Mix (see above)
2 large eggs

- Preheat the oven to 180°C/160°C (fan)/350°F/gas mark 4. Line a 12-hole muffin tin with 10 muffin cases.
- Stir the flour, baking powder and salt together in a bowl. Pour the milk into a jug and stir in the vanilla extract. Set aside.

- In a separate bowl and using an electric hand mixer, cream the butter and sugar until light and fluffy. Add the chai latte mix and beat until well combined. Add the eggs one at a time, beating well after each addition.
- Add half the flour mixture and beat on a low speed until just combined. Pour in half the milk and vanilla and mix until smooth. Repeat until all the flour and milk is used up.
- Spoon the batter evenly into the muffin cases, filling each case to about two-thirds full.
- Bake for 15–18 minutes, until the cakes are golden brown on top and an inserted skewer comes out clean.
- Leave to cool in their tin for 10 minutes before turning out onto a wire rack to cool completely.

VANILLA BUTTERCREAM ICING

85g unsalted butter, at room temperature
45ml milk, at room temperature
¾ teaspoon vanilla extract
375g icing sugar

- Place all the ingredients in a bowl and, using an electric hand mixer, beat on a low speed until combined. Scrape down the sides of the bowl, then beat on a medium-high speed for a further 30–45 seconds until the icing is smooth and lump-free.

DECORATE

a little Chai Latte Mix (see above), for sprinkling on top

- Ice each cupcake with the vanilla icing and sprinkle the top with some chai latte mix.

MINT CHOCOLATE CHIP LOAF

I love mint chocolate, so both this recipe and the one for the Chocolate Mint Slice on page 224 really appeal to me and I found it very hard to stop eating them when we first made them at the bakery. This rich loaf cake would be amazing on a cold winter afternoon decorated with as many After Eights as possible!

Makes one 900g loaf, serving 8–10

MINT SUGAR

100g fresh mint leaves
45g golden caster sugar

- Place the mint leaves and sugar in a food processor bowl and pulse until the mint leaves are fine.

MINT LOAF

75g dark chocolate (70% cocoa solids), broken into small pieces
100g self-raising flour
15g cocoa powder
½ teaspoon baking powder
155g unsalted butter, at room temperature
120g soft light brown sugar
145g Mint Sugar (see above)
2 large eggs
130ml milk
1½ teaspoons peppermint extract
1 teaspoon vanilla extract
95g dark chocolate chips (70% cocoa solids)

- Preheat the oven to 180°C/160°C (fan)/350°F/gas mark 4. Lightly grease a 900g loaf tin and line with parchment paper or a loaf tin liner.
- Put the 75g of dark chocolate into a microwaveable or heatproof bowl and gently melt, either in the microwave in short bursts or over a pan of lightly simmering water on the hob. Leave to cool slightly.

- Stir the flour, cocoa powder and baking powder together in a bowl, and set aside.
- In another bowl and using an electric hand mixer, cream the butter, brown sugar and mint sugar together in a bowl until light and fluffy. Add the eggs one at a time, making sure the first one is well incorporated before adding the second. Pour in the melted chocolate and beat until well combined.
- Add the flour mixture and mix until it just comes together. Then pour in the milk, peppermint and vanilla extracts and beat until you have a smooth batter.
- Fold in the chocolate chips with a spatula, then pour the batter into the prepared loaf tin.
- Bake for 40–45 minutes, or until an inserted skewer comes out clean.
- Allow the loaf to cool in its tin for 15 minutes before turning out onto a wire rack to cool completely.

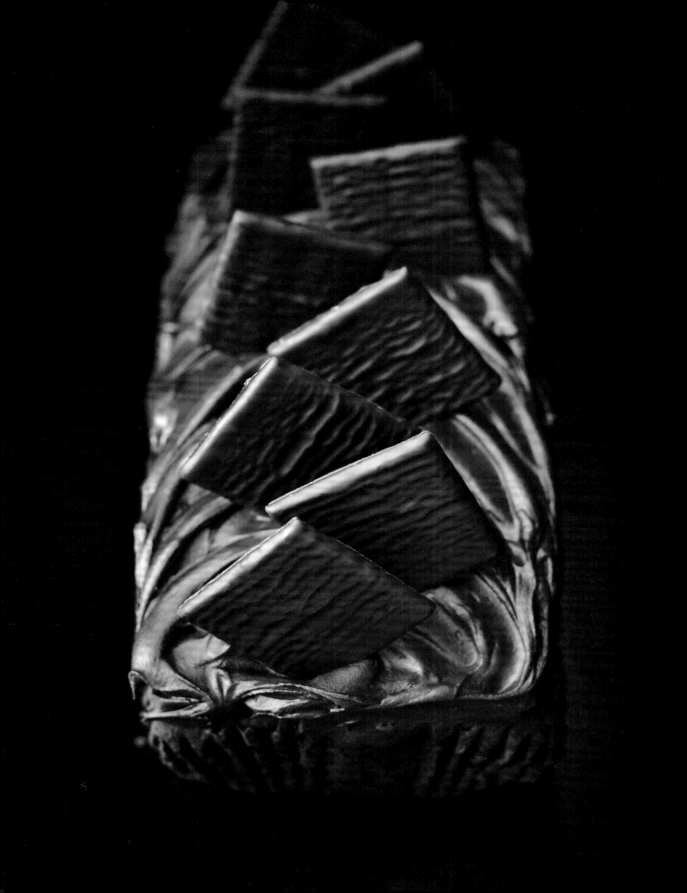

MINT GANACHE

90g dark chocolate (70% cocoa solids), broken into small pieces
120ml double cream
20g fresh mint leaves
1 teaspoon peppermint extract

- Put the chocolate into a heatproof bowl and set aside.
- Pour the cream into a small pan over a low heat and slowly bring to the boil. Once the cream starts to boil, remove from the heat and add the mint leaves. Allow the mint to infuse into the cream for 30–60 minutes until the cream cools down.
- Strain the cream to remove the mint leaves and squeeze out all the excess cream from them. Then return the cream to the pan, add the peppermint extract and bring to the boil again. Once the cream starts to bubble, pour it directly over the chocolate. Stir with a spatula or wooden spoon until the chocolate has melted and the mixture is smooth.
- Set aside to cool until it reaches a spreadable consistency.

ASSEMBLE

After Eight mints

- Ice the top of the loaf with the mint ganache, then top with a few (or a lot of) After Eight mints.

INDEX

10 9 8 7 6 5 4 3 2 1

Square Peg, an imprint of Vintage,
20 Vauxhall Bridge Road,
London SW1V 2SA

Square Peg is part of the Penguin Random House
group of companies whose addresses can be found
at global.penguinrandomhouse.com.

Penguin
Random House
UK

www.vintage-books.co.uk

A CIP catalogue record for this book is available
from the British Library

Photography by Stuart Ovenden
Design by Sandra Zellmer
Prop styling by Alice Whiting and Martha Swift
Food styling by Daniel Harding and Lisa Chan

ISBN 9780224100762

Printed and bound in China by C & C Offset Print Co., Ltd

Penguin Random House is committed to a sustainable
future for our business, our readers and our planet.
This book is made from Forest Stewardship Council®
certified paper.

MIX
Paper from
responsible sources
FSC® C008047